DISCARD

SHELTON STATE COMMUNITY
COLLEGE
JUNIOR COLLEGE DIVISION
LIBRARY

CO-AWS-533

12.00

E   Goldwater, Barry Morris
744
.G57   Why not victory?: A fresh
1980   look at American foreign
          policy

DATE DUE			

WHY NOT VICTORY?

By Barry M. Goldwater

THE CONSCIENCE OF A CONSERVATIVE

WHY NOT VICTORY?

BARRY M. GOLDWATER

WHY NOT VICTORY?

A FRESH LOOK AT AMERICAN FOREIGN POLICY

GREENWOOD PRESS, PUBLISHERS
WESTPORT, CONNECTICUT

Library of Congress Cataloging in Publication Data

Goldwater, Barry Morris, 1909–
    Why not victory?

        Reprint of the 1st ed. published by McGraw-Hill,
    New York.
        Bibliography: p.
        Includes index.
        1. United States--Foreign relations--1945–
    I. Title.
    [E744.G57 1980   327.73   79-28300
    ISBN 0-313-22316-5 lib. bdg.

Copyright © 1962 by Barry M. Goldwater.

All rights reserved. This book or parts thereof may not be
reproduced in any form without written permission of the
publishers.

Reprinted with the permission of McGraw Hill Book Company.

Reprinted in 1980 by Greenwood Press, Inc.
51 Riverside Avenue, Westport, CT 06880

Printed in the United States of America

10 9 8 7 6 5 4 3 2 1

TO MY CHILDREN
AND ALL THE CHILDREN OF THE WORLD
TO WHOM TOMORROW BELONGS

CONTENTS

WHY NOT VICTORY?

INTRODUCTION

FOR THE AMERICAN CONSERVATIVE, there is no difficulty in identifying the day's overriding political challenge; it is to preserve and extend freedom. If concern for this challenge were not felt by conservatives there would be no need to articulate our position, to argue for it, or to argue against those who disagree. There would be no need for this book, whose purpose is to extend in words the concern felt by one conservative about the forces in the world and our nation which are working against the preservation and extension of freedom.

If I were alone in this feeling, one might charge me with being overly obsessed with an unwarranted concern for our freedoms, but there is no sensation of aloneness in this. To the contrary, there is the growing certainty that

13

the majority of the American people share commonly in it. Particularly I detect this concern among the youth of America wherever I meet them: in the schools and colleges and universities, in the early years of business, in the professions, in labor and politics. They are sensitive to the dangers that threaten freedom everywhere.

Young people are discovering that, contrary to what they might have been told in school, conservatism is not dead. Conservatism is a natural philosophy which recognizes man as having a spiritual and a material side, and that the two are intertwined. One cannot be affected without a reaction taking place in the other. Consequently as the focus is placed on the material side, the spiritual side weakens. From this comes a weakening of man which can today be seen in our apathy toward crime in all categories, in man's greater and greater reliance on a government for the solution of his daily problems, and in man's reluctance to face the real dangers loose in the world today. Conservatism being a natural philosophy, the young have little trouble recognizing its value. It is not difficult to show them that changing the nature of man by edict is impossible and that trying to change the pattern of our economic system by applying to it theories tried and found wanting in the past simply does not make good sense.

Some people believe that conservatism is applicable only to economics. In their minds conservatism has become a sort of exercise in bookkeeping, which it isn't at all. Its truths can be applied to every problem and situation which we have before us today and which will crop up in the future. It is my hope that this book will demonstrate this to the readers' satisfaction in the field of foreign affairs.

When I first reached Washington some ten years ago, the radical press thought it was insulting enough merely to refer to a man as a conservative, but today they reluctantly recognize the ascendancy of conservatism to the point that they now feel it necessary to add the words "right-wing" or "arch" followed by a hyphen to the word "conservative." I have laughingly told them that when they drop the hyphen they will have admitted the legitimacy of conservative philosophy.

We older people who call ourselves conservative have been neglectful in our duties in not having devoted more time to discussing with the younger generations what we feel is essential to our survival as free people—and the traditional values that are the foundation of our way of life. We have been wishfully hoping that the tides would turn without any force being exerted by ourselves to cause this to happen. But the young know this cannot be and they have begun the movement that will create the momentum needed better to demonstrate conservative thought and application.

We have been too engrossed in a battle of semantics with the opposition and too often with ourselves. Time has been wasted on ridicule instead of explanation, time in which the sands of freedom have kept on dropping slowly through the glass. But the young will not waste time nor will they allow time to waste them. They are not repeating the failures of the generations which have preceded them by lack of action.

Years ago the Goldwater children slept on an open porch which was our bedroom. We would be awakened before sun-up in the winter by the long, lonely whistle of the train coming down from Prescott. Morning after morning, day after day, year after year came the welcome sound. I can hear it still. It was a sound of people going someplace. People still do, but the sound is different.

I remember that sleeping porch well, for many a hot afternoon it had absorbed so much of the desert sun's heat that sleep was an impossibility when night came. Then came a great invention, the electric fan. I can remember my father bringing it home and the men on their way from work stopping to marvel at this new device. I can still see it flopping back and forth, interrupted in its arc only long enough for its rudder to change course. Today we cool ourselves to any desired temperature by the mere flick of a switch, and once it has been flicked the marvel of automation takes control of our homes' weather. The sun is just as merciless, the heat that that old fan fought is still outside the window, but the sound of the fan is only a memory—the sound of trying to stay cool.

My children will not hear those sounds, just as I rarely heard the clup-clup of horses' hoofs down the main street. My ears were more attuned to the first backfires of automobiles. Then when I saw man turn to the sky for travel, I learned to fly. I still fly but, again, the sounds have changed. The roar of an engine with open stacks and whirling propeller and the perpetual sound of wind rushing around a goggled head have been replaced by the subdued rumble of a jet engine well behind the cockpit, with a canopy to deny one the sound of the air.

Change will be always with us in our material life, but I suggest that man's desire for freedom will never change and he will seek it and fight for it in the future as he has in the past. I further suggest that change for its own sake— just any change no matter how wild and untested—is not necessarily good.

A sound conservative philosophy can and must be extended into the area of foreign affairs just as it must be applied at home. Such a conservative approach would be based at least in part on the lessons of the past. It is wrong to equate modernism with experimentalism, with turning our back on the past, with radical internationalism, with a scorn for tradition. In foreign policy, as well as in every other aspect of our lives, traditional values must continue to have influence.

That is why I ask, *why not victory?* Once upon a time our traditional goal in war—and can anyone doubt that we are at war?—was victory. Once upon a time we were proud of our strength, our military power. Now we seem ashamed of it. Once upon a time the rest of the world looked to us for leadership. Now they look to us for a quick handout and a fence-straddling international posture.

I am not calling for a return to the naked power politics of the nineteenth century. I am not asking that we declare hot war on Russia or turn a deaf ear to the pleas for help from destitute nations. I am willing to be as "modern" as anyone—as long as "modernism" does not constitute a debasing of our traditional values. But if to be "modern" I must accede to policies that would turn the foreign affairs of the United States over to the United Nations, disarm our great military machine, welcome Red China to the Community of Nations, give away our food and technical skills to the so-called neutralist nations and get nothing in return—if this is what is meant, then indeed I am not modern and never want to be.

As this book goes to press, Lt. Col. John Glenn has just descended from space to light our lives with a fierce new pride and patriotism. If we can consider this fine young man and his extraordinary accomplishment as symbolic of America's future, then we have reason to hope that this nation may turn away from the weakness and tragic blunders of the past to lead the Free World back to a position of unrivaled power and pride.

In proceeding with this book I want to acknowledge the invaluable help of many people living and dead who have contributed to my thinking, writing, and speaking. They would be my uncle Morris, who taught me the ways of Jefferson; my mother, who showed me the advantages of being a Republican; my close friend Stephen Shadegg, who collaborates with me on a column, "How Do You Stand, Sir?"; Brent Bozell, who was the guiding hand of my last book; Bill Buckley, Bill Rickenbacker, Russell Kirk; Michael Bernstein of the minority staff of the Labor and Public Welfare Committee, who has been my friend and right arm on legislative matters for ten years; his assistant, Ray Hurley, and another of my own, Bill Seward. Add to this the team which helps me on the Floor during debate and in committee during hearings; my administrative assistants, past and present, Henry Zipf, Charles Farrington, Dean Burch, Ted Kazy; the man who does research and writing for me, Tony Smith; my secretary, Edna Coerver, who translates and puts into correct grammar my miserable typing; my staff, without whose help nothing would ever get done; and friends too numerous to name. Among these would be Denison Kitchel, Phoenix attorney, who has advised me on the legal aspects of the Connally Amendment, and Dr. Gerhart Niemeyer of the University of Notre Dame, whose views on the Communist War have proved an invaluable help in my research. These are but a few of those who provided me with the crutches I so badly need. There is no feeling of weakness in admitting my need for this help. The fight for conservatism requires the thoughts and the efforts of many.

Furthermore, I have my hands full working in the Senate, working for my country, my state, and my party. The way I look at it, polishing my prose is not something on which I can spend a lot of time, as enjoyable as that is. It is a rare and unbusy man in this field who can do all of this himself. The homework was mine to do and I wrote the first draft on the Norwegian freighter M.S. *Burrard* of the Fred. Olsen Lines during a trip from San Francisco to London. And I enjoyed every moment of it. But for the proper expression of the result of that labor, I, for one, depend on those I have mentioned—helpers, ghosts, call them what you will. They are an indispensable part of politics and writing.

ONE

THE WORLD-WIDE COMMUNIST MENACE

WHEN WORLD WAR II ended Americans breathed a sigh of relief, celebrated, and began an unsuccessful search for peace. War returned to its distant place in our lives and, except for those whose loved ones never came back or returned with the scars of war, the experience had not been a harsh one. More people were employed at higher wages; new homes, new cars, a higher standard of living was everyone's lot. Once again Americans had gone through a war fought on distant shores of other lands and once again we had won on the field of battle. But, as we had done before, we lost those gains on the smooth surface of the peace table. We weren't aware of or didn't read the signs put up at Teheran, Yalta, and Potsdam that pointed to a third world war which would

21

take the stage even before the last act of World War II was finished.

This was soon to be known as the "Cold War," a term we accepted as applying to a war of "no shooting," a war which in some way would have no effect on our lives. At first we alone had the secret of the atom bomb as our protection—but not for long. In the Old West, the six-gun was called the equalizer: it made all men the same height and the same strength. The atom bomb and its offspring, the nuclear bomb, have become the six-guns of today's world.

We are now spending as much money for armament as we spent during World War II. Yet there are still Americans who do not understand that we have been at war these past sixteen years with an enemy who has never hidden his objective of destroying us and all other people who cherish freedom. As a people we have become like the man who suspects he has cancer but will not see his doctor for fear his suspicion be confirmed. One cannot talk with his fellow Americans—individually or in groups—without sensing the apprehension with which they view today's happenings. But at the same time, one comes to feel that they do not want to know the truth. All of us recognize some symptoms of trouble, but we are not dealing with the disease itself. The disease is communism, a cancer that is world-wide and that shows symptoms within our own boundaries.

There can no longer be any doubt about our situation in today's world: we are at war; not a cold war but a real war—we can call it the Communist War, war of a more deadly nature than any we have fought before. We may well be now engaged in a phase of World War III which if we lose will mean the end of freedom as we know it. But we need not lose this war, either elsewhere in the world or here at home; and it is my hope that the suggestions I will make in this book, in admittedly limited fields, will help point the way to victory. Victory is the key to the whole problem; the only alternative is—obviously—defeat. As a people, through our government, we must begin this effort by proclaiming to the Communists that we intend victory as our lot and that we will shape our every move to accomplish it. Once having made this decision, which should have been made long ago, we can design our national strategy to achieve it.

The first thing a military man in combat wants is an estimate of the situation—the nature of his enemy. In the case of the Communist War this information should become the property of every American of every age. It should be taught about in the schools, discussed in the churches and in the other places people gather; it should be the topic of meeting after meeting of service clubs, women's clubs, and business organizations. Americans today must know their enemy as well as they must know their own history and the strengths of their own governmental, social, and business systems. They should be constantly explaining these strengths to other Americans as well as to friends and critics abroad. When communism is shown side by side with the way of free people, communism cannot win.

For too long we have closed our eyes to the naked truths of communism. Following Stalin's death, we eagerly accepted the statements of wishful thinkers who predicted a new era of lessening tensions.

At the Geneva summit meeting in July, 1955, even so

wise and worldly a leader as President Eisenhower was misled into proclaiming the "dawning of a new day in world relations." But our goals and those of communism are irreconcilable.

In 1961, Charles Nutter of International House, New Orleans, outlined before the English-Speaking Union in Kansas City, in a way that everyone can understand, what communism really is:

Communism is an international conspiracy which has restored slavery to the world. . . .

It has captured, enslaved, and exploited a billion people against their will, and plans to capture the remaining two billion people on earth.

It has destroyed freedom, liberty, independence, human rights and dignity wherever possible.

It has interfered and intervened times without number in the domestic affairs of free nations.

It has established deceit, dishonor, destruction, death and disaster as recognized, accepted, and necessary instruments of an international policy.

It has destroyed the sanctity and usefulness of solemn international agreements and treaties by deliberately scrapping these at will to serve its purpose.

It has spread Communist imperialism throughout the world, creating millions of lackeys of this Red imperialism.

It has made man the "producing animal" which Karl Marx labeled him.

It has made communism the greatest threat and enemy of peace in the world while professing, in Communist doubletalk, to be peace-loving and solicitous of human welfare.

It has starved, murdered, or otherwise destroyed at least

a hundred million human beings to advance false economic and political doctrines repugnant to man. . . .

It has challenged and seeks to destroy religion and belief in a Higher Being all over the world.

Communism has destroyed freedom of religion, of the press, the right to vote, to own property, to work where you please, to organize into labor unions, the right to assemble, protest, and change government by will of the people, has destroyed government by consent of the governed, freedom of education, and the right to live in freedom.

Finally, communism has destroyed honor in the world it controls, and substituted dishonor as accepted policy in its national and international relationships.

These are clear, inescapable truths about our enemy. Yet, there are those among us who still suggest that we can coexist with this philosophy. These people are the hard core of those who, whatever their reasons, will not and do not recognize the real threat of the enemy without. Yet so recently as January, 1961, the new Communist manifesto said in part "peaceful co-existence of states does not mean renunciation of the class struggle. Peace is a true ally of socialism, for time works for socialism and against capitalism. The policy of peaceful co-existence is a policy of mobilizing the masses and launching vigorous action against the enemies of peace."

But the enemy of peace is communism; the Communists make no secret of this. Nevertheless, in spite of the outspoken intentions of our enemy and his known successes to date, in spite of his calling almost every shot, we are forestalled from victory by those whose heads rest blissfully in the sands of yesteryear and who refuse to recognize that while the basic principles of war have not changed, our enemy now sees peace as war and war as peace.

At this moment in history lessening of tensions is impossible. It is because the United States and the USSR stand for two antithetical concepts of the nature of man. Our commitment is to things of eternal value—we believe in truth and honor and justice and the liberty and dignity of man. The Russian doctrine is dedicated, in the words of Stalin, "to the destruction of all capitalist society. . . . The individual is of no importance except as he serves the State. . . . The end is justifiable by any means. The individual has no rights. The individual is only a cipher. Let me tell you the democratic concept of man holds that each man is a sovereign being. This is the illusion, dream, and postulate of Christianity."

Forty years ago a handful of Communists began to implement their plans to destroy the social, economic, and political establishments of the free world. Today the Communist masters rule a billion people—a third of the world.

It is absolutely necessary for our survival that we, as individuals and as a nation, understand that every Communist statement, every action, every feint at some other country, every domination of some other government is but a step in the long march to dominate the United States. The United States, with our free republic and our free economy, is the barrier communism must overcome before its ultimate objective of absolute world domination can be accomplished.

The total military, scientific, economic, and social resources of the Communist world are therefore dedicated to our destruction. Though Khrushchev is reported to have told his Chinese counterpart that a military attack on the United States will no longer be necessary because communism is winning everywhere throughout the world without it, this hardly makes communism any the less dangerous.

An enemy which has steadily increased its domination over other peoples and other lands by warfare, rebellion, treason, and subversion can no longer be ignored by thinking Americans. And yet, we still go about our everyday business, being good neighbors, providing comforts for our families, worshiping God, and stubbornly refusing to admit the enormity of the conspiracy which has been created to destroy us.

A conflict which has cost us more than five hundred billion dollars in the last ten years is hardly a normal condition of world affairs.

And yet, because Americans genuinely long for peace and have no selfish ambition to dominate the rest of the world, we hopefully and unrealistically accept every suggestion that the hostility against us can somehow be mitigated by purchase or appeasement.

During the years since World War II there have been sporadic outbursts of Communist activity and aggression such as those in Berlin, Poland, Korea, Hungary, Lebanon, Cuba, and Laos. The American people have reacted momentarily, but our general concern has not lasted long. Failing to understand the real significance of these events and the pattern of which they are a part, we have dismissed each one as just another unexplainable act of the unexplainable Communists and then gone on with our daily tasks.

Let us look at the result.

Is Soviet influence throughout the world greater or less than it was in 1945? Is Western influence greater or less than it used to be?

In answering these questions, we must consider many more factors than merely whether Communist troops have crossed over into territories they did not occupy before, whether disciplined agents of the Cominform are in control of governments from which they were formerly excluded. The success of communism's war against the West today does not depend alone on such spectacular and definitive conquests. *Communist success may mean merely the displacement of Western influence.*

The Soviets understand, moreover, what we appear not to: that the first step in turning a country toward communism is to turn it away from the West. Thus, typically, the first stage of a Communist takeover is "neutralizing" a country. (The realistic Russians never for one moment tolerated the suggestion that satellite countries on the borders of Russia could be permitted to remain neutral.) Yet spokesmen for the free world are now proclaiming that all we ask is for the emerging nations to adopt a neutral stance.

The second stage of Communist takeover retains the nominal classification of "neutral," while the country is turning into an active adherent of Soviet policy. This may be as far as the process will go. The Kremlin's goal is the isolation and capture, not of Ghana, for instance, but of the United States—and this purpose may be served very well by countries that masquerade behind a "neutralist" mask, but are in fact dependable auxiliaries of the Soviet

Foreign Office. What difference does it make to them if Nkrumah is not a disciplined Communist, so long as both his public policies and his intrigues accelerate Soviet ascendancy in Africa?

The list of recent major Soviet successes is hardly reassuring:

Seven years ago French Indo-China, though in trouble, was in the Western camp. Today North Vietnam is overtly Communist; Laos is teetering between communism and pro-Communist neutralism; for all practical purposes, Cambodia is neutralist.

Indonesia, in the early days of its Republic, leaned toward the West. Today Sukarno's government is heavily laced with admitted Communists, and for all of its "neutralist" pretentions is a firm ally of Soviet policy.

Ceylon has moved from a pro-Western orientation to a neutralism openly hostile to the West.

In the Middle East a short while ago, Iraq, Syria, and Egypt were in the Western camp. Today the Nasser and Kassem governments are adamantly hostile to the West, are largely dependent for their military power on Soviet equipment and personnel, and in almost every particular follow the Kremlin's foreign-policy line.

A few years ago all Africa was a Western preserve. In the struggle for the world between communism and freedom that vast land mass was under the domination and influence of the West. Today, Africa is swerving violently away from the West and plunging, it would seem, into the Soviet orbit.

Latin America was once as "safe" for the West as Nebraska is for Republicans. Today it is up for grabs.

Cuba has become a Soviet bridgehead ninety miles off our coast—a condition we appear powerless to do anything about. Castro's triumph has been such a shot of adrenalin to latent anti-Americanism everywhere south of us that one sees it like an ugly specter spreading through Central and South America. And in every country there—save the Dominican Republic, whose funeral services we recently arranged—Castroism or anti-Americanism prevents the governments from espousing the North American cause unqualifiedly.

Only in Europe have our lines remained firm—on the surface. But the streams of neutralism are running strong, notably in England, and also in Germany.

It is clearly and sadly obvious that Soviet influence *is* greater and far more dangerous than it was in 1945. Just as discouraging is the other side of the coin: Western prestige and influence have declined during the same period— the result of our uncertain national policies and of the single-minded, single-goal drive of world communism.

The overwhelming reason for the Communist success to date has been the Communist ability to "think big" and move boldly in their efforts to dominate vast areas of the world, plus their absolute dedication to their single objective.

The Communists do not view war as a "hot" or "cold" affair. To them conflict is a continuing action everywhere —in the open, behind the scenes, in men's minds, on battlefields, in conferences.

Communist political warfare, remember, is waged both insidiously and in deliberate stages. The Communists seek to undermine Western power on battlefields where the nuclear might of the West is more or less irrelevant—in backwoods guerrilla skirmishes, in mob uprisings, in parliaments, in clandestine meetings of conspirators, at the United Nations, on the propaganda front, and at diplomatic conferences, preferably at the highest level.

Great publicity was given in 1961 to the Russians' claim that they put a man in orbit and returned him safely to the earth. Our scientists applauded this achievement as a step forward in man's ongoing effort to understand and penetrate the mysteries of the universe. But to the Russians this was no scientific experiment: this was an act of war—a calculated effort to secure an advantage which might be exploited militarily.

Every shipload of food the Russians dispatch to a foreign country, every Russian technician sent overseas, every cultural exchange, every international conference is an integrated part of the calculated grand strategy of communism.

At the moment this Russian strategy does not contemplate armed conflict, but Khrushchev has never abandoned the possibility of fighting to gain his total end. The free world, much more sensitive to the horrors of nuclear war and influenced by a small group of intellectuals who refuse to face reality, is gradually accepting the notion that anything is better than fighting. Surely this is among the reasons that history during the last sixteen years has recorded an endless succession of free-world defeats. I happen to be one who believes that armed conflict may not be necessary to defeat communism. But I am convinced that when we renounce the possibility of armed conflict *in advance* before each new Communist thrust, we are courting disaster.

All Communist activities, whether they are called military or political, seek to advance the main strategic plan of world domination. To understand the total Russian approach it is necessary only to reread the passage Lenin underscored in his personal copy of Clausewitz' *On War*:

> If war belongs to policy, it will naturally take its character from thence. If policy is great and powerful, so also will be the war. And this may be carried to the point at which war attains to its absolute form.
>
> It is only to this kind of view that war recovers unity, and only thus can we attain the true and perfect basis and point of view from which great plans may be traced out and determined upon.
>
> There is upon the whole nothing more important in life than to find out the right point of view from which things should be looked at and judged of and then to keep to that point, for we can only apprehend the mass of events in the unity from one standpoint, and it is only the keeping to one point of view that guards us from inconsistency.

This is a very remarkable passage from a most remarkable book. We know that Lenin was attracted to this statement, and it is not difficult to see that this concept has become the basis for Communist planning.

Clausewitz saw war in its "absolute" form. The Communists have translated this into a master strategic plan in which every action is carefully calculated to further the one objective of ultimate victory: world domination. Time has relatively little importance in this plan.

Since the Communists believe time is with them, they have no imperative to achieve victory this year or next. Their plan does not even require absolute success in every effort. They are willing to accept some defeats if by allowing minor setbacks they can advance the over-all objective.

Certainly as one studies Russian strategy of the past forty years he recognizes that above all the Communists have been guided by their objective. Its two-pronged strategy includes (1) enlargement of land holdings until the time that they become, by mass of land, the absolute power in the world and (2) application of their philosophy to the governments and economies of those lands. It is impossible to separate the two; one cannot come without the other in the total accomplishment. Furthermore, direct acquisition of land by Russian military conquest has not been necessary since World War II—infiltration and corruption visited upon established governments have succeeded where, in the past, only military intervention would have been successful.

For the last forty years, however, the Western world has steadfastly refused to recognize the nature and continuation of this constant conflict. In those few isolated instances in which the West has reacted properly with power, we have denied communism an immediate victory. This has not deterred them, because by sticking doggedly to one point of view they have practiced a consistency which defies discouragement and defeat.

Until 1950, America had never lost a shooting war. Within the past ten years we have suffered repeated defeats, not because we lack the power or the ability, or even the will to resist Communist aggression but because we have failed to recognize the stark reality of the *existence* of Communist aggression.

We still possess abundantly the material resources, the courage, the technical and scientific know-how to defend our freedom. But there can be no victory for freedom unless, and until, the men and women of this free land demand that our government have done with accommodation of the enemy and adjustment to his purposes.

Bombs and missiles will not stamp out communism. Ideas are only defeated by better ideas or by the endless repetition of the same ideas—a deceptive consistency at which the Communists excel.

This means that we must announce to the world as the Communists have so long been doing that defeat is unacceptable; that we believe our cause is just and that, if necessary, we are prepared to fight and to die in defense of freedom. Recognizing this, we must then act accordingly by laying out our own master strategic plan to stop the ideas of communism with the better ideas of free men.

I would suggest that we analyze and copy the strategy of the enemy; theirs has worked and ours has not. In viewing their success we must recognize the possibility of war as it relates to our national policy or objective. Unless we see this instrument in its proper perspective, we are likely, with the terrible implications of a shooting war today, to proceed with the same timidity that has marked our foreign relations for the last forty years. Once having decided on a national objective (and I am convinced that this now has to be *victory* over communism, the only course open if we are to protect the security and integrity of America and eventually of the world), we must proceed with the development of an over-all strategy to accomplish it. While war is the last of the instruments to be employed as a means by which this national objective can be attained, it must nevertheless be considered.

We must engage in the *economic warfare* for which we are admirably equipped if we do not fritter away our economic strength by destroying our capitalistic system.

We must improve our techniques in *political warfare*, which we can do if we will concentrate on the reaching of our main objectives and not let ourselves be pulled by the nose into every little corner of the world by the Communists.

And one of the most important and immediate improvements which we need desperately is in the field of *psychological warfare*. In this area we should be supreme. Our ability to sell material goods to our people and to the world is phenomenal, but we have not been successful in selling the American idea to the world. No sane person can argue that communism has provided freedom for people or that socialism has given a high standard of living to the people who now live under its bureaucracy. Neither can any sane person argue that we in America have not, through our free institutions, provided both a level of personal freedom never before enjoyed in history and the material goods that are part of a high living standard. It is in the realm of psychological warfare that we can make the most immediate and effective gains; our entire genius must be applied to the problem.

Recalling the advice of Clausewitz not to deviate from our objective once we have established it, we must form a team of the various agencies of our government whose charge will be carrying out the strategy. The State Department and all its subagencies must maintain constant liaison with the military, the Executive, the Congress, so that every move aimed at the attainment of our objective will be fully coordinated. We cannot long afford the luxury of one department going off on its own with its action not related in any way to the furtherance of our goal of *victory*.

We must recognize this war as a *war*—not a cold one, but the *Communist War*—and we must win it.

TWO

AMERICA'S POWER
—USE AND MISUSE

IF OUR FOREIGN POLICY has had a hallmark since the end of World War II, it has been inconsistency. We have marched resolutely up the hill of power and then timidly allowed ourselves to be maneuvered onto a toboggan back down that slope. We have made strong pronouncements of intention based on our power, then refused to use that might to augment the words. When we have spoken strongly and acted in character with the words, we have been successful.

At those moments, we experienced the respect due the greatest power on earth beginning to manifest itself, only to see it smitten down with a subsequent act of weakness inspired by indecision, doubt, and confusion.

On the whole, no one can say convincingly that our

foreign policy since the Second World War has consistently gained our ends, even when those ends were clearly defined. We have lived in an almost perpetual state of crisis with the determined Communists, who never for a second have doubted or questioned their aims. We have watched them as one watches the weaving head of a cobra while they have subverted, betrayed, and manipulated wherever the opportunity presented itself and, being awed, we have been confused.

What course, then, should we take if we are determined to stop communism and eventually replace the whole destructive idea of communism with our free and productive one?

To answer this question, I must begin by setting down some assumptions with regard to our national objectives. I do not mean to suggest that everyone will agree with them. I mean, however, that I do take them as valid and that everything I say on this subject is set against their background.

Assumption 1. The objective of American policy must be to protect the security and integrity of Americans and thereby help establish a world in which there is the largest possible measure of freedom and justice and peace and material prosperity. I speak of "the largest possible measure" because any person who supposes that these conditions can be universally and perfectly achieved—ever—reckons without the inherent imperfectability of himself and his fellow human beings.

Assumption 2. Attainment of the largest possible measure of freedom, justice, peace, and prosperity is impossible without the prior defeat of world communism. This is true for two reasons: (1) because communism is both doctrinally and in practice antithetical to these conditions and (2) because Communists have the will and, so long as their power remains intact, the capacity to prevent their realization. Moreover, as Communist power increases, the enjoyment of these conditions throughout the world diminishes by that much and the possibility of their restoration becomes increasingly remote—becomes, at the end of the road, a cause that is absolutely and tragically and irretrievably lost.

Assumption 3. It follows that victory over communism must be the dominant, proximate goal of American policy. Proximate because there are more distant, more "positive" ends we seek, goals to which victory over communism is but a means. But victory is dominant in the sense that every other objective, no matter how worthy intrinsically, depends on it and thus must defer to it. Peace is a worthy objective but if we must choose between peace and keeping the Communists out of West Berlin, then we must fight. Freedom, in the sense of self-determination, is a worthy objective, but if granting self-determination to the Algerian rebels entails sweeping that area into the Sino-Soviet orbit, then Algerian freedom must be postponed. Justice is a worthy objective but if justice for Bantus entails driving the government of the Union of South Africa away from the West, then the Bantus must be prepared to carry their identification cards yet a while longer. Prosperity is a worthy objective, but if providing higher living standards gets in the way of producing sufficient weapons to be able to resist possible Communist aggression, then material sacrifices and denials will have to be made. It may be, of course, that we can safely seek such objectives and at the same time assure a policy designed to overthrow communism; the important point here is that when conflicts arise they must always be resolved in favor of achieving the indispensable condition for a tolerable world—the absence of Soviet-Communist power.

The question now remains whether we have the resources for the job we have to do—defeat communism—and, if so, how those resources ought to be used. This brings us squarely to the problem of *power* and the uses a nation makes of power. This is the key problem in international relations; it always has been, it always will be. Further, the main cause of the trouble we are in today has been the failure of American policy-makers, ever since we assumed free-world leadership in 1945, to deal with this problem of power realistically and seriously.

During the Presidential campaign of 1960 the absurd charge was made by Mr. Kennedy and others that America had become—or was in danger of becoming—a second-rate military power. Any comparison of over-all American strength with over-all Soviet strength reveals the United States not only superior, but so superior both in present weapons and in the development of new ones that our advantage promises to be a permanent feature of the United States–Soviet relations for the foreseeable future.

Having often searched for a graphic way of impressing this superiority on those Americans throughout the land who have doubts and misgivings, I discovered that Jameson Campaigne has expressed it particularly well in his *American Might and Soviet Myth*. Suppose, says Mr. Campaigne, that the tables were turned and we were in the

Soviets' position: "There would be more than two thousand modern Soviet fighters, all better than ours, stationed at two hundred and fifty bases in Mexico and the Caribbean. Overwhelming Russian naval power would always be within a few hundred miles of our coast. Half of the population of the United States would be needed to work on farms just to feed the people." Add to this the unrest in the countries around us where oppressed people would be ready to turn on us at the first opportunity. Add also a comparatively primitive industrial plant which would severely limit our capacity to keep abreast of the Soviets.

If we look at the situation this way, we can get an idea of Khrushchev's nightmarish worries—or, at least, of the worries he might have if the West were disposed to exploit its advantage.

As a case in point, let us not forget that, until a year or so ago, Khrushchev had been telling the people of his own and the Iron Curtain countries that *no one* could ever penetrate the borders of Russia. Then one day one of our aircraft, the U-2, was forced to land in Russia, and Mr. Khrushchev had to acknowledge the fact that for four years American pilots had been flying at will over the heartland of Russia, at seventy to eighty thousand feet, at relatively slow speeds, photographing Russian terrain and Russian military installations. The Russians had been powerless to stop us. They still are.

The rulers of the Kremlin are determined to master the world. They have said so, for forty years. If, at any given point during the last fifteen years, the Kremlin had felt that Russian military forces could be certain of winning a military contest with the United States of America and that the time was ripe, you can be sure we would have been at war. You can be equally sure that on the day communism feels itself militarily superior to the United States, war will begin.

Thus, our own first resolve must be to retain—and enhance—our military superiority. Mere equality in this field will not do. Since we could never match the Communists in manpower, our equipment and weapons must more than offset their advantage in numbers.

What sorts of weapons?

Commencing early in human history, the country that has controlled the dominant means of transportation at the time has been the world power. The first great powers were those that exploited the rivers of Asia. Their methods spread through the Red Sea and into the Mediterranean, and Egypt and Greece became in turn world powers because they had mastered navigation of that inland sea. Then Portugal became the leader of the world as she mastered the oceans, to be followed by Spain and then England.

England is the classic example of transportation affording world power to a nation. England was master of the seas; for about one hundred years, by judicious use of sea power during that period, England kept the world from going to war.

Since World War II, the United States has been the leader of the world. Why? Not because we have the strongest economy (which we do), not because we are necessarily the best-educated people (which we are), but because we have been and still are the masters of the air.

The West, particularly the United States, possesses the

greatest military power in the world today. It is the fact
of this power which has kept the uneasy peace over the
last fifteen years. It is this power, this military supremacy,
which will keep the peace in the coming years. We must
jealously preserve that power advantage, enhance it by
constant development of new weapons and new techniques
—not to wage war against Soviet Russia but to wage an
effective peace.

The power I refer to is that of the Strategic Air Command and its gigantic potential for retaliation. Our SAC
bombers and our missiles, always on the alert, are enough
to deter any world leader in his right mind from making
aggressive moves in our direction. That is not to say that
we should stand pat with the armaments we have. We must
—unfortunately—continue to build bigger and better
weapons until the Communist menace has subsided.

In some quarters the theory of massive retaliation is
being undermined by those who would place their reliance
in the exclusive development and use of conventional
weapon systems. That these systems assuredly have their
place in our defensive inventory cannot be denied, and
that we have been relatively weak in that area is a matter of
public knowledge. Indeed, we must be ready to fight all
sorts of wars—brush fire as well as nuclear. But to *replace*
a supersonic bomber with a rifle and a tank would, in my
opinion, be disastrous. What is needed as we apply the
concept of power is a combination of nuclear and conventional weapons with a variety of methods of delivery. SAC
should remain the deterrent force it has been and our
ground—and air—support forces should be equipped with

an assortment of nuclear tactical weapons and those we commonly term "conventional."

What of the uses we are to make of our power? History shows powerful nations that have used their strength to preserve the peace and to preserve a climate in which their ideals and their concepts of government have flourished. Have we followed this wise and valid course?

No, we have not.

Laos and Cuba are the tragic results of weakness in our dealings with the Communist leaders, a softness that has resulted in a constant acquiesence to their gruff freedom-killing demands. This is the result of an attempt to buy the world for our side rather than to gain its respect by strong action for freedom.

The loss of Laos and Cuba to communism, if that be their fate, is not simply the tragedy of people going into slavery; it will also be the disaster of losing friends at a time when friends are needed.

Strong words alone do not wave off the Russian leaders. They understand and they respect strength and strength alone. The sadness is not that we are weak militarily or economically. The sadness lies in our consistent refusal to orient our foreign policy to our true strengths.

I suggest that the United States and her allies go on the offensive. We can't win merely by trying to hold our own. In other words, in all our dealings with Communist or neutralist nations, we *must not* be on the defensive. We must go on the offensive with what we have, knowing that what we have in America now is better than man has ever devised before in the history of the world.

We have had opportunities—clear invitations to plant our influence on the other side of the Iron Curtain. There was the Hungarian Revolution in October of 1956, which we praised and mourned but did nothing about. There was the spectacle of Korea, where, with victory in our hands, we chose instead the bitterness of stalemate. Only in one instance have we moved truly purposively and effectively to dislodge existing Communist power: in Guatemala, in July, 1954. We moved decisively to effect an anti-Communist *coup d'état*, and there is no need to apologize for what we did. We served our national interests, and, in so doing, we saved the Guatemalan people the ultimate misery. If there are doubts, ask the Hungarians. Or the Cubans.

Think long on Guatemala, for this is our single full-fledged triumph. We have held the line in some places—in Lebanon, in Berlin, in the Formosa Straits—but nowhere else in the far-flung battle for the world have we *extended* the influence of the United States and *advanced* the cause of freedom.

Last December in Berlin, I saw with my own eyes the latest result of our hesitation and weakness—the notorious wall between East and West. I know that hindsight is easier than foresight but I have yet to talk with a Berliner or an American commentator who was on the spot or a knowledgeable military man who has not expressed the opinion that had the West destroyed this wall brick by brick as it was being constructed, the East Germans would have retired from the border and today there would be no wall. The wall is not so important as a physical barrier as it is as a great propaganda victory for the Communists.

They wanted to seal off East Berlin—so they did it. The West did not raise a hand. The rest of Europe stands by and shrugs resignedly. They have seen another show of Communist strength.

We may take it, then, that unless radical changes are made on our side, the situation will progressively worsen until the United States is at bay—isolated and besieged by an entirely hostile world. What changes? One thing, but it is everything: We are going to have to shed the attitudes and strategies of weakness and start behaving once again like a great power. We must act from strength to gain respect, not prestige.

In this we must recognize that the affairs of nations are not determined by good-will tours, alms-giving, gestures of self-denial, rehabilitation projects, and discussion programs. The affairs of nations are determined—for good or for evil—by *power*.

On July 15, 1953, the United States, at the request of President Carmille Chamoun, landed a brigade of Marines in Lebanon to help prevent a revolt inspired by the United Arab Republic intent on overthrowing Chamoun's democratic government. President Eisenhower complied immediately with President Chamoun's request on the theory that Lebanon in revolt would certainly fall victim to Communist infiltration. He acted wisely. Three months later, Chamoun's control having been stabilized, the Marines withdrew without ever firing a shot in anger. American power, in this situation, was used promptly and to excellent effect as it has been so seldom since the end of World War II.

The Soviet Union has not gotten where it is today

through the attractiveness of its doctrines and practices. It has set its sights on distinct targets—geographical areas or power centers which it means to infiltrate and eventually conquer—and then turned the full weight of its national power, plus the power of the international apparatus it controls, on these particular targets. The United States has never viewed the world struggle in quite this way—as essentially a military campaign in which a commander isolates his objective, marshals his forces, and takes it!

We have rather proceeded on the assumption that virtue was its own reward and that our only real goal is to make the world love us and perceive our virtue.

Moreover, we entered this supposed contest for world approval with a kind of guilt complex. Perhaps the dropping of the atom bomb on Hiroshima had something to do with it. But more probably the cause lies deep in America's past, in our traditional attitude toward power politics. Having been brought up on childish myths about the evils of European power politics, Americans felt uneasy when the rights and duties of being the greatest power on earth suddenly fell upon them at the end of the Second World War. In order to prove that we were not selfish, ambitious, warlike, as our predecessors in power were, we began to lean over backward and to gear our policies to the opinions of others. There are notable exceptions—as when, for example, we have submitted to the imperatives of self-defense: in Greece, in Korea, in the Formosa Straits, in Berlin. But in theme and thrust and motive American foreign policy has been primarily an exercise in self-ingratiation.

I am, of course, oversimplifying the case but not exaggerating it. Call into question any aspect of American policy, and the argument you will hear after the others have been laid to rest is some variation of the world-opinion theme. Foreign aid, deference to the United Nations, and cultural exchange programs, exchange visits of American and Soviet functionaries, summit conferences, the nuclear-test ban, advocacy of general disarmament, anti-colonialism, the refusal to intervene early enough in Cuba, the establishment of world government—all of these programs and postures have a single common denominator: an effort to please world opinion. Indeed, many of these policies are frankly acknowledged by their proponents to be contrary to the immediate interest of the United States; yet they must be pursued, we are told, because of the overriding importance of having the world think well of us. This sluggish sentimentality, this obsession for pleasing people, has now become a matter of grand strategy; it has become no less than the guiding principle of American policy, leading us—for all the good intentions it implies—to national and international disaster.

And what does the world admire anyway? Strength, courage, and ingenuity! When was the United States more admired than during the Berlin Airlift? After the Russians blocked our road access to Berlin on April 1, 1948, we and the British started the air shuttle which was to last eighteen months until September 30, 1949, and which was to bring to West Berlin the staggering sum of 2,343,301 tons of food and coal. In almost 300,000 flights seventy airmen lost their lives—but the blockade was broken and the free world was inspired by this display of power and skill. All this effort only retained the *status quo,* a danger-

ous stalemate in Berlin. It prompts one to wonder what
we might be able to do in the way of driving communism
backward if, instead of merely responding defensively to
their moves, we applied that power and ingenuity to offensive gestures.

There are three fairly plain reasons—aside from the fact
that this is a substitute for a real foreign policy—why deference to world opinion is so harmful to American interests.

First, it is self-defeating because the very admiration and
respect we covet is denied to us the moment we go out and
beg for it. Human beings and nations being what they
are, altruistic behavior by a great power is never honored
beyond the first flush of surprise that it has happened.
The would-be beneficiaries of our concessions and self-
denials soon construe them as weaknesses and want more.
Does anyone seriously suppose, for instance, that our generous decision to permit the Panamanian flag to fly over
American territory in the Canal Zone will placate the
Panamanian nationalists? The gesture is bound simply to
whet the mob's appetite and transfer its sights to bigger
targets.

Second—in terms of propaganda impact—a long history
of trying to prove your good faith when it had never really
been open to question has the paradoxical effect of raising
doubts about your good faith. When we, with our record,
enter into a propaganda contest with the Kremlin, with its
record—when we try to match Soviet professions of love of
democracy and peace or hatred for armaments and colonialism, we invite the world to look upon us as it looks
upon the Soviets, as propagandists with something to hide.

We lose our natural advantage over the Soviets, established by our history and our deeds. By not taking the superiority of ourselves and our cause for granted, we forbid others to take it for granted, and we find ourselves forced to make a new plea before the bar of "world opinion" every time *Pravda* lets go with a new blast.

Third, in gearing our policies to world opinion, we have chosen the one standard most vulnerable to manipulation by our enemies. What is world opinion? Who participates in the poll? How do you measure it? To begin with, the term is a misnomer. When we talk about world opinion, we are not talking about a consensus of two billion human beings, most of whose opinions we know literally nothing about; we are talking about that tiny segment of the world's population that can make itself heard. Intellectuals, journalists, the organizers of street mobs. But these real sources of world opinion are traditionally prime targets for Communist infiltration. Because of their critical importance in the kind of struggle we are now witnessing, these directors of opinion are precisely the targets at which Communist agitators and propagandists have been aiming over the years. It is thus only natural that Communist influence in such areas should be far out of proportion to communism's real strength in the world. When we allowed world opinion to determine our policy toward Trujillo and Syngman Rhee, we were in effect giving our mortal enemies a voice in our own councils.

For too long we have permitted the tail to wag the dog —deferred to the ineffectual and even harmful policies of other nations, often in a fashion detrimental to our own national interests, even to our national security. It is time that we ceased fearing to give offense to so-called neutralists, and unpredictable friends, and even the enemies who are resolved upon our destruction. In doing so, we have earned not their respect but their contempt, and have convinced them that they can push what they mistakenly regard as their national interests at the expense of ours, at the expense of the security of the free world itself.

It is time we made clear to the rest of the free world that we are at least as necessary to their survival as they are to ours—and if we are not afraid to speak the truth, even more necessary.

The dogged determination with which some of our leaders cling to the concept that the loyalty of others can be purchased with our dollars should have received a rude jolt when Nehru announced to the world the feelings of the neutral nations assembled at Belgrade late in 1961. Russia had, during that conference, resumed nuclear testing and had exploded huge nuclear devices not once but on several occasions during that time, but the sense of the statement released by Nehru blamed not the Russians but the United States! This is surely a display of the age-old doctrine of man respecting and—in this case—fearing strength. The "neutrals" who joined in the expression were peoples who have benefited by our lavish gifts of American dollars and technical assistance, but when the chips were down it was the military power of Russia they respected, not the Santa Claus attitude of the United States.

A striking example of the kind of accomplishment which gains world-wide respect and admiration would be Russia's spectacular feats in space. A whole year before the United States, Russia put two men in orbit.

As the name of Major Gagarin became a household word

around the world, Russia's prestige in science and technology shot ahead of that of the United States. And more
than simply a scientific endeavor, this was the Communist
world flexing its military muscles: the same extraordinary
thrust which catapulted Major Gagarin into orbit can
send deadly missiles winging thousands of miles toward
targets in New York, Washington, Chicago, and Los An-
geles.

I ask you to consider a ridiculous thought: how would
Russia's "world prestige" have been affected if, instead of
spending billions on space technology to send Major
Gagarin aloft, she had invested that money in tractors for
India, fertilizer for Ghana, and medical supplies for Vietnam? My answer would be that her prestige in the world
would be considerably lower than it is today. That intan-
gible "world opinion"—which is more a matter of respect
than it is love—would not be smiling at Soviet Russia
with the same intensity.

The plain fact is—and we either fear or are ashamed to
acknowledge it—that if we go down, the whole free world
goes down with us. If we survive, all other nations can
have a reasonable hope for their own survival. Actually, if
they genuinely desire freedom and independence, the
United States is their only hope, and we must impress
on them this fact. Starting from this fundamental premise,
a policy which reflects such an attitude will inspire precisely the respect that we have been trying to buy, and
dispel the contempt we have bought instead.

THREE

U-2

AN AMERICAN U-2 high-altitude recon-
naissance aircraft aircraft piloted by a thirty-year-old
civilian named Francis Gary Powers crashed near Sverd-
lovsk, just east of the Urals, some twelve hundred miles
inside the Soviet Union on May 1, 1960, just two weeks
before the much-heralded summit conference in Paris. No
other single incident has pointed up so many facets of our
precarious position today.

(As this book goes to press, Powers has been released
and, on the wings of Mr. Khrushchev's phony dove of
peace, has come flying home to the United States. Disclosure of further details pertaining to the case will make
it all the more fascinating and important. But nothing can
change its basic outline or diminish its value as an object

lesson. It would be doubly tragic and ironic if we were to consider Powers' release as a serious Communist peace overture. Nothing could be further from the truth. In some way which we must quickly ascertain, this gesture of amnesty, offered at this moment, fits into Khrushchev's master plan for ultimate world domination.)

By the time the first tumult and shouting had slackened, back in May of 1960, these things—among others—had occurred:

The Kremlin had seized the incident and begun milking it of every propaganda advantage it offered, and there were many. Moscow's stories flew thick and fast—and conflicting, but all used to Moscow's advantage. It did not appear to make any difference that the landing blew to smithereens the USSR's carefully nurtured myth of its own air superiority.

Washington had issued contradictory statements at several levels—we never heard of Powers or U-2, we knew them both well; we would continue the flights, we would discontinue the flights—treating the world at large to a generous sampling of our lack of coordination and purpose in handling matters of delicacy in the sharpening Communist War.

The world press had had a field day reporting, commenting, and speculating. Powers pleaded guilty, confessed, and was sentenced to "ten years deprivation of freedom." A picture of his "suicide needle" appeared on front pages the country over. His mother and father and wife were thrust into the limelight. Even his salary for the dangerous mission became a matter for speculation.

"World opinion" was afforded opportunities to swing in

many directions—few of them tending toward credit for
the United States.

The stage was set. Mr. Khrushchev noisily scuttled the
Paris summit conference the very day it opened, on May
16, by refusing to begin the talks until President Eisenhower publicly apologized.

But far more important, this period revealed basic principles behind the sensational news events.

It let us see clearly the uses of strength—and its misuses.
It disclosed our lack of sophistication and agility in the
handling of such a "hot potato," and showed clearly and
unmistakably the duplicity of the Communists and the
naïveté with which we approach Russian diplomacy. It
demonstrated our clear technological lead. And it offered
an interesting example of the power exercised on our foreign-policy formation by journalists.

When Nikita Khrushchev assaulted Dwight Eisenhower
in Paris shortly after the U-2 incident, employing the
vulgar, uncouth profanity for which he is well known,
Americans were shocked. Yet a wave of not too thinly
veiled criticism developed in the United States which attempted to suggest that President Eisenhower was responsible for the failure of the summit conference. No recent
aspect of world affairs has been subjected to so thoroughgoing an analysis or such educated second-guessing as was
applied to that attempted conference. Much of the com-
mentary at the time seemed to me, to say the least, ill advised.

Since most of the discussion of the collapse of that
summit meeting begins or ends with the capture of the U-2
and its pilot, it seems to me we should place this event

in proper perspective before we commence discussion of the lessons here for us.

To begin with, I have had from the first some misgivings about the Committee on Foreign Relations' inquiry into the summit meeting. I certainly am casting no aspersions on the competence of that Committee, but I felt that most of the hidden facts of the U-2 episode were of a military or intelligence character and should therefore remain unpublicized. More important, I felt that great mischief could be done by an investigation which proceeded under the assumption that there was an American "failure" at Paris, and that those "responsible" must be brought to book. Nevertheless, the inquiry was undertaken.

The decision to investigate flowed directly out of the contention that the American government bore a large part of the blame for the collapse of the Paris talks, as I have suggested. This contention was based in turn on the theory that two American acts—Eisenhower's assumption of responsibility for the U-2 flights, and the statements by him and Secretary of State Herter implying the flights would continue—left Khrushchev no choice but to break up the summit. This theory was adopted by several authorities: by Khrushchev himself; by Adlai Stevenson; and by a number of lesser American personages. The copyright, however—at least by virtue of first usage—belongs to Mr. Walter Lippmann, who spelled it out in his column five days before the summit blew up. By that token, if Mr. Lippmann is not the architect of a policy criticism, he is at least its American prophet and ardent supporter.

Mr. Lippmann is not an ordinary writer. He is, in addition to being a columnist, a political force. Some people seem to be impressed by the solemnity of his writing

(Heaven knows it has that) and others say he is wise. Whatever the reason, he is quoted with great deference. His words carry undoubted weight in strategic quarters. I say these things, not in criticism of Mr. Lippmann or to suggest there is anything sinister about his influence, but by way of explaining why I think his theory important enough to discuss.

Mr. Lippmann's campaign to picture the United States as the offending party in pre-summit diplomacy began on May 12, 1960. That was the day after the weekly Presidential news conference at which the then-President Eisenhower affirmed his own responsibility for the flights and implied that they would continue. The President's policy, Lippmann advised, "is quite unworkable." He continued in this key passage:

"To avow that we intend to violate Soviet sovereignty is to put everybody on the spot. It makes it impossible for the Soviet government to play down this particular incident because now it is challenged openly in the face of the whole world. It is compelled to react because no nation can remain passive when it is the avowed policy of another nation to intrude upon its territory."

Lippmann belabored the President for not having taken what he called "the conventional way out which Mr. K offered." The "conventional" response, Mr. Lippmann explained, would have been "to disclaim responsibility for the U-2 flight, and to accompany the disclaimer, as Senator Kennedy has quite properly suggested, by a formal and perfunctory expression of regret." The President's failure so to lie and so to apologize was, Mr. Lippmann concluded, "a fatal error . . . an irreparable mistake."

If these assertions are correct—and if Stevenson and

Kennedy were correct in endorsing them—then Khrushchev was fully justified in blowing up the summit. That is to say, if it is true that it was "impossible" for Mr. K to play down the incident, and that in fact the Kremlin was "compelled" to react violently in order to preserve its self-respect, then it is also true that we, not the Soviet Union, bore the responsibility for the collapse of the Paris talks.

Note, too, that Khrushchev himself fully appreciated the value of this argument. It was his central propaganda theme for weeks. He used it in Moscow before he left for the summit meeting. He used it in his opening statement at the Elysee Palace. He used it again in the course of his vile tirade against the President during a Paris press conference. The argument was the cornerstone of Khrushchev's official report to the Soviet Union:

"After the Soviet disclosure of the U-2 flights, we resolved to do nothing that would prevent the United States President from getting out of this embarassing predicament. We even declared that the United States President hardly knew about and certainly did not approve such actions and that evidently the hotheads from the Pentagon and Allen Dulles were to blame. But Eisenhower did not take advantage of the opportunity granted him. He declared that the spy flight had been approved by him and made with his knowledge. . . . That is when it became obvious that the purpose of the aggressive actions by the United States was to torpedo the summit meeting."

The Lippmann line and the official propaganda line of the Soviet Union is incompatible with some of the major facts of the case.

First and most obvious, it was not the United States but the Soviet Union that made an international incident out of the U-2 episode. The subsequent breakdown of the Paris talks will never be understood unless this initial event is kept clearly in mind: that Khrushchev deliberately chose, in a flamboyant speech before the Supreme Soviet on May 5, to publicize the American flights and his claim that one of our planes had been shot down. The magnitude of this decision to draw public attention to the flights and the high stakes for which he was playing can only be appreciated in terms of the great risks Khrushchev was running in admitting Russian vulnerability.

For many months Soviet propaganda had traded heavily on the claim of Soviet military invincibility. The claim that the USSR was as strong or stronger than the United States was a prime tool in Soviet propaganda attempts to intimidate the uncommitted nations, our allies, and ourselves. The Kremlin knew, of course, that the claim was false. Soviet leaders knew, among other things, that for four years American intelligence aircraft had roamed at will through Communist air space—over China as well as over Russia. The Kremlin knew that it had neither the rockets nor the aircraft to prevent this activity. During these four years, however, Khrushchev did not make a public issue of the flights—for the obvious reason that to do so would be to expose the astonishing weakness of the Soviet air defenses.

On May 5, 1960, however, the Kremlin abandoned this policy. When one of our planes crashed (it was definitely not shot down from cruising altitude, as Moscow claimed), Khrushchev chose to blow up the matter into a full-scale international incident, thereby admitting to the world that Soviet air frontiers were vulnerable.

Let us postpone examining what Khrushchev hoped to accomplish by creating this incident—and note here simply that it was he, not we, who created it. It was therefore assuredly not impossible for the Soviet government to play down this particular incident. Having created the incident, Khrushchev quite obviously had no desire to play it down until he had achieved the purpose for which he had originally played it up! Khrushchev is not known as a frivolous man. We may be sure he did not create an international crisis that involved great damage to his country's prestige and the possible loss of his own power, only to let it die—as Lippmann, Stevenson, and Kennedy suggest he would have—by accepting President Eisenhower's disclaimer of responsibility and regrets. Khrushchev had other fish to fry, as his conduct in Paris was soon to make clear.

The second fact that contradicts Lippmann's theory is that Khrushchev refused to go ahead with the summit— even after President Eisenhower announced the U-2 flights had been discontinued and would not be resumed. Before the Paris meeting Lippmann had written that his only criticism was that the President had made spying our "avowed" policy. (The further recommendation—that the President should have apologized—did not find its way into the Lippmann pieces until after Khrushchev had demanded an apology in Paris.) It was the avowal that had made it "impossible" for Khrushchev to play down the incident. The President disavowed the policy: a promise to discontinue a past policy. And still Khrushchev blew up the summit. My personal judgment is that it was unwise to have disavowed the policy once it had been avowed. The point, however, is that once it was disavowed, there was no further excuse under the Lippmann theory for Khrushchev to refuse to hold the summit talks.

Now suppose the President had done exactly what his leftist critics wanted him to do. Suppose he had taken "the conventional way out which Mr. Khrushchev offered," and had made some such statement as this:

"The U-2 flight was conducted without my knowledge or permission, and the United States Government regrets that it took place."

Does anyone seriously think—in the light of what had already happened and of what was to follow—that Khrushchev would have let the matter drop at that? Having persuaded the President to eat that much crow, he would surely have tried to force him to eat the whole bird. It is not difficult to imagine Khrushchev's rejoinder to such a statement by Eisenhower:

"We are delighted to learn that President Eisenhower had no part in the infamous spy mission, and that he has not known anything about these aggressions against Soviet territory that have been carried on for four years by his subordinates. It is therefore with great sorrow that the Soviet government finds itself unable to accept the United States' statement. If the President is not master of his own house, what assurance have we that these flights will stop? Surely it is intolerable that these international bandits should remain at large. The Soviet government cannot be satisfied with anything less than public exposure, trial, and punishment of those who perpetrated these outrageous crimes. We know in the interest of peace the United States President will take steps to assert his constitutional authority," and so on.

Remember: Once it was clear that Khrushchev was determined to exploit the plane incident, and once it was clear that he was in possession of physical proof that the flight took place, nothing could have been more foolhardy than for the President to have tried to deny it, or to have pretended he did not know what was going on, or to have apologized for it.

This brings us to a point that has disturbed many people on both sides of the aisle. Would it not have been better, they ask, for the United States simply to have remained silent during Khrushchev's tirades in Moscow? Couldn't we in that way have avoided compromising the reconnaissance operation, and also have avoided the embarrassing public acknowledgment that we were violating international law? Wasn't there something unprecedented and unusual in our behavior when we decided to talk openly about our spy policy?

I believe the answer to these questions is to be found—once again—in Khrushchev's original decision to make capital of the U-2 incident.

Can anyone remember a previous instance in modern history in which the chief of state of a major power has gone before his country's parliament to make a public exposure of another great power's intelligence activities and coupled that exposure with a demand for public satisfaction? Spy incidents, to be sure, have been publicized before. When a Colonel Abel—or any one of scores of Soviet spies—is apprehended, our Justice Department announces it to the press; speeches commenting on the arrest may be made in Congress; the prisoner is tried by the courts and he may be convicted. But does the President of the United States, in such an instance, go before Congress, wave documents in the air purporting to prove Abel's guilt, and demand before the world that Khrushchev explain whether he was personally involved in sending Abel over here? Such a performance would, indeed, break all conventions. Chiefs of state do not publicly address one another about spy operations—unless one of them is deliberately using the incident to achieve some other purpose. This is precisely what Khrushchev did: It was *he* who broke the conventions by insisting that the American government make a public accounting for a spy operation, the proof of which was already in Soviet hands.

Once Khrushchev had decided on this extraordinary course, the United States had no choice but to react in kind. Once Khrushchev decided to make spy operations a factor in international diplomacy, the United States had to assume that his real purpose in creating the incident was *diplomatic* in nature; that the decision to publicize the U-2 flight and the summit meeting were, in other words, inextricably intertwined.

What, then, was Khrushchev's purpose? What were the high stakes for which he was willing to sacrifice the myth of Soviet air invulnerability? (Paradoxically, the fact that this question must still be asked is evidence that Khrushchev has partially achieved his purpose.) What is the mystery here? Why do we fumble for an answer that fairly leaps out at us?

Khrushchev wanted Berlin. Khrushchev had told the

world that if Berlin were not given to him, he would take it. Khrushchev became convinced, as the summit meeting drew near, that Berlin was not going to be given to him—that the United States had decided to call his bluff.

Khrushchev thereupon decided to torpedo the conference under circumstances that would camouflage the fact that his bluff had been called.

The U-2 mishap came at a time when it could be seized upon as a weapon with which to blackmail the United States into making last-minute concessions on Berlin or, if that failed, used as an excuse for scuttling the conference.

Because of the West's firmness on Berlin the Soviet Union was on the threshold of a major diplomatic defeat. It was Khrushchev's last-minute strategy to prevent that defeat, or, if it could not be prevented, to throw sand in the world's eyes so that the defeat would not be recognized or appreciated. Thanks to the steady nerves of our government at the critical moment, Khrushchev failed in his efforts to force concessions on Berlin.

But I feel that Khrushchev's alternate objective—that of diverting attention from the fact his bluff was called—achieved realization. For far from celebrating the technical and strategic accomplishment of the U-2, we still cringe at the recollection. We are haunted by the doubts of those spiritless creatures in our midst who ask, plaintively, whether we dare to win. Instead of taking to heart the lesson of those weeks, and proclaiming it to the world, we are—ourselves—trembling before it. We cannot quite accept, even now, the moral of the ordeal—that firmness pays off.

Significantly, responsible spokesmen for the other nations of the free world have correctly catalogued Khrushchev's exploitation of the U-2 reconnaissance flight as no more than a timely excuse for an action the Russian Communists had intended to take before Khrushchev left Moscow for Paris.

Victories will not always come so easily for the West: we may not always be able to avoid shooting. But when a happy event does occur and we are vouchsafed such a triumph, let us recognize what has happened. Let us not collapse of shock for having taken a strong stand.

And I, for one, do not shed tears over the collapse of that Paris summit meeting. I have consistently opposed summit meetings on the grounds that the only progress they can produce is progress toward Communist domination of the world. Either summit meetings must fail for having achieved nothing, or they must fail for having yielded to the Communists something of value to the West. The only summit meeting that can succeed is one that does not take place.

The Communists never entertain the idea of a summit meeting, much less participate in one, unless they hold the high cards. They come to the conference table with two things in mind—possible real or propaganda advantage to them. And when we come to that table seriously seeking agreements in areas of contention, we automatically concede them the advantage because they don't care about agreements. Even assuming that some form of agreement is achieved at a summit meeting, what is there in the lessons of the past to make us think the Communists would honor such an agreement? The Russians have entered into literally hundreds of agreements, treaties, and determinations with other countries in the past forty-five years, but they have never felt obliged to honor any of those agreements which happened to interfere with their world-wide revolutionary designs. Summit meetings definitely are not the way to peace in the Communist War. Let us never forget that.

Actually, every American can find pride and reassurance in the knowledge that American ingenuity and industry were able to produce an aircraft capable of penetrating the solid wall which surrounds the activities in our enemies' heartland. Contrary to the almost-open-door policy we have adopted toward the wanderings of Communist agents through the secrets of our offensive and defensive capabilities, until the advent of the U-2, prying similar information from Russia had been almost impossible for us. Instead of suggesting that we hang our collective heads in shame over the incident, we should have been admonished to hold them high in the pride that was rightly ours. Here were two fine opportunities to blow our own bugle in a tune that the world would have understood: first that we could overcome the physical difficulties of gaining needed knowledge, and second that the Soviet claim of air superiority was a pure myth. The proper playing of these two psychological aces could have benefited in great measure the position of the United States and, carried to their fullest, could have dimmed the advantages gained by Russia as she exploded the Paris meeting.

(To me, another psychological opportunity was missed by not making it plain to the world that, had the shoe been on the other foot, had a Russian reconnaissance plane been discovered flying over our country, had we so desired, we could have destroyed that craft at her cruising altitude.)

Let us not lose sight of the fact that this remarkable U-2 aircraft is capable of efficient operation at altitudes above 60,000 feet; that it has been, and will continue to be, extremely useful in the performance of missions other than high-altitude reconnaissance. Above all, let us remember that this plane represents the state of development in the United States aircraft industry six years ago and we can reasonably expect that technological advances have now made the U-2 obsolete, by our standards. Yet what we must class as an obsolete aircraft successfully penetrated the Russian defense system. And this flight was not a happy accident or a one-shot activity. For many months the U-2 operated on the defense perimeter of the Western world, engaging in high-altitude air sampling.

The congressional inquiry into the administration's handling of the U-2 plane flight and the collapse of the summit talks in Paris might far more profitably have spent its time and money in an attempt to understand fully that truth which so many Americans have ignored: Russia is responsible for the Communist War; Russia is the aggressor nation determined to conquer the world; peace for Russia means defeat for the United States, and no amount of appeasement or soft talk will dissuade the Russians from their determined effort to rule the world or destroy it.

That is the heart of the lesson.

FOUR

CUBA

NOW LET US LOOK at a danger that is real and close at hand, the conversion of Cuba into a bastion of communism ninety miles from our shores and in close proximity to our Latin American friends.

Today freedom is dead in Cuba. The dark night of totalitarianism has descended, obliterating human dignity, cheapening human life, destroying all semblance of human rights. It has set a reign of terror over our neighbors to the south. It has substituted a harsh, all-powerful Communist state for the revolution's promises of democracy. It has replaced reason with the firing squad. It has ridiculed and persecuted religion. It has abandoned property rights and substituted government confiscation.

American foreign policy has produced some notable

failures in the past thirty years. Until recently these mistakes have borne their bitter fruit in Southeast Asia, in Europe, in the Middle East, in Africa. But all of these lands are separated from our homeland by a distance sufficient to dull our sense of urgency and our fear of immediate contingent penalties.

Cuba, just off our mainland, presents quite a different situation. The average American citizen, preoccupied with earning a living and with family responsibilities, can with some justification ignore the implications of the establishment of a Communist government in, say, Laos. But no American can ignore the deadly serious situation resulting from the establishment of a Communist-dominated government on the island of Cuba.

Fidel Castro, at the tender age of thirty-two, ousted Dictator Fulgencio Batista from power in January of 1959. He formally became Premier on February 13, and a wave of executions (557 actually recorded) and thousands of imprisonments followed in the very first year. Land reforms, nationalization of industries, the training of militia, a friendly visit to the United States by Castro, and loud denials of any Communist sympathies followed quickly.

Yet only a few months later Castro was grabbing American sugar refineries, encouraging Communist revolts in Haiti, Nicaragua, and the Dominican Republic, negotiating economic and diplomatic ties with Russia, and mounting a vicious hate campaign against the United States.

Americans shook their heads in bewilderment and looked around for leadership.

Discovering the truth about Castro shouldn't have been

an impossible, or even a difficult task for the United States government with its far-flung intelligence resources. From the very beginning there were voices, some of them highly placed and important voices, that warned of communism among Castro's top leaders. For example, there was never much serious doubt that the rebel leader's brother, Raoul, was a thoroughgoing Marxist. And there certainly was no doubt about the notorious Che Guevara. At the very least, the warnings should have been thoroughly investigated and the findings given to the American people.

Our people needed this information to guide their reactions to something that looked like a wholesome revolutionary action but actually was evil at the core. It is part of our American decency and good will that makes us want to support the "underdog"; that makes us think that a man like Castro—a man leading a revolt against a dictator—is a good man and a liberal after the fashion of those great Americans who fought for their own independence back in 1776. Now this is a fine, warm-hearted tendency on the part of the American people, and none of us would ever want to see it disappear. But its misuse, particularly in the case of events in Cuba since Castro, has been tragically confusing.

I might add that part of the responsibility rests with certain segments of the American press. It is impossible for me to understand why a writer for one of the most respected newspapers in the United States—*The New York Times*—would persistently defend a Communist regime like Castro's merely because he had met its architect and been impressed by Castro personally. Certainly such a paper as the *Times* has a responsibility far beyond the impressions of one representative on a subject of vital interest, not only to our national survival but to the welfare of the entire Western Hemisphere.

Here is President (then Senator) Kennedy's comment on Castro in his book *The Strategy of Peace.*

> Just as we must recall our own revolutionary past in order to understand the spirit and the significance of the anticolonial uprisings in Asia and Africa, we should now reread the life of Simon Bolivar, the great "Liberator" and sometime "Dictator" of South America, in order to comprehend the new contagion for liberty and reform spreading south of our borders. On an earlier trip throughout Latin America, I became familiar with the hopes and burdens which characterize this tide of Latin nationalism.
>
> Fidel Castro is part of the legacy of Bolivar, who led men over the Andes Mountains, vowing "war to the death" against Spanish rule, saying, "Where a goat can pass, so can an Army." Castro is also part of the frustration of that earlier revolution which won its war against Spain but left largely untouched the indigenous feudal order.

The evidence is strong and getting stronger that our State Department was informed of Castro's Communist leanings before and during his invasion of Cuba. There is ample testimony to suggest this in hearings before the Judiciary Committee of the Senate on June 12, 1961, by former Ambassador to Mexico Robert C. Hill.

On page 799 of this document, in answer to a question from Mr. Sourwine, "Now, what intelligence did you send or forward to the Secretary of State dealing with the matter of Castro's Communistic connections?," the testimony proceeded as follows:

Mr. Hill: "There was a continuous flow of information from the Embassy, Mr. Sourwine."

Mr. Sourwine: "Beginning when?"

Mr. Hill: "As soon as I arrived in Mexico in 1957. . . ."

Mr. Sourwine: "You say the tenor of this intelligence at all times, from 1957 forward and growing stronger as the years progressed, was that Castro was surrounded by Communists and influenced by Communists?"

Mr. Hill: "That is correct."

What is perhaps even more shocking was Ambassador Hill's further testimony about favorable reports of Castro going back to Washington from State Department and intelligence sources. "In my opinion," said Mr. Hill, "many of those documents were slanted in favor of Fidel Castro. I recall one, for instance, that dealt with Castro's first year in power. I thought it treated Castro in a much kinder fashion than this infamous character deserved."

Of course, now that Castro has proclaimed his communism to the entire world and boasted that he covered it up in the early days of his revolution, everybody is falling in line. The State Department has issued a White Paper and the most rabid pro-Castro partisans in the American press have pulled in their horns. But my contention is that it shouldn't have been necessary for many Americans to have to adjust their feelings in the light of Marxist-Leninist admissions from Castro. We should have been told in the very beginning by the United States government the exact nature of the so-called "uprising" in Cuba. I believe that it could have been done with a more serious and less prejudiced investigation by our intelligence branches.

The situation in Cuba is not entirely unlike the situation that existed there in the days of tyranny that preceded the Spanish-American War. Let us consider the attitude of our government when the Cubans were writhing then under the boot of Spanish imperialism. Let us consider the patriotic temper of our people as it flamed forth in the interest of hemispheric freedom at that other time when a European power dominated our doorstep.

In the 1800s the heavy hand of Spain still crushed the little island of Cuba with the same tyranny and greed and selfishness that had marked the Dons' colonial policy in the Western Hemisphere from the days of Alva, Pizarro, Cortes, and De Soto. The Spanish government paid no attention to the new spirit which the United States, by its example, was fostering throughout the Americas. It did not recognize the Monroe Doctrine of 1823 as a policy which might apply to its own disreputable rule in Cuba. It paid little heed to the strong cultural and economic ties growing up between Cuba and the great Republic to her north. In short, Spain followed a blind policy of calculated cruelty and oppression in the handling of her Cuban colony —ruthlessly suppressing every spark of independence or individualism that flickered among the starving, beaten-down population of the island.

Even as it does today, Cuba in the late 1800s confronted the United States with a problem and a menace. For seventy years the possession of Cuba by Spain—and Spain's handling of that possession—had been a source of distress to the United States. The methods of the government, its treatment of the people, the continual restlessness and unhappiness of the Cubans, the severe economic exploitation of the people—all this violated the deep-seated American spirit of fair play and concern for human decency. Starvation, exploitation, destruction, and desolation were ruining one of the fairest islands in the world—an island which, from the time the Spaniards had discovered and occupied it, had never had a chance to develop its resources or lift its people above the ranks of feudalism. And all this was going on right on our doorstep under the protection of a foreign power.

The chief villain of this early Cuban story was another warlord, a General Weyler, who was the Spanish Governor of Cuba and whose name became synonymous with brutality to all Americans in the days preceding the turn of the century. It was General Weyler who devised one of the most cruel, most inhuman concentration camps in all history. He issued an order which gave all the country residents of Cuba eight days to move into areas of fortification but denied them the right to transport food. The result was calculated starvation of hundreds of thousands of Cubans who ordinarily subsisted on what they could raise. Famine and disease rode unchecked throughout all of the areas of Cuba where guerrilla forces had concentrated their opposition to Weyler's tyranny. And the heaviest sufferers were the women and children.

When what the *reconcentrado* order of General Weyler actually meant in terms of human lives and suffering dawned on the American people their indignation was instantaneous. There were demands for intervention, for action. But these demands were ultimately shouted down by a chorus of appeasers. The appeasers said: "This is a foreign matter. It's none of our business what the Spaniards do. If we take any action it might run the risk of war."

It is important to remember that American indignation in those days stemmed almost entirely from humane considerations for the Cuban people. The Spaniards were not insulting and ridiculing the United States as Castro does today. They weren't conspiring with enemies of our way of life and our system of government as is the Castro government in Cuba today. They weren't seeking to extend an ideological concept which would subvert American interests throughout the Western Hemisphere. They were just brutally guilty in their treatment of the Cuban people of a conduct so inhumane that the United States was finding it difficult not to act in the interests of decency, order, and justice.

There was some official procrastination, and this perhaps was understandable. America was not a very old nation and not yet fully over the effects of a brutal and bloody Civil War. Spain was an old hand in the family of nations, knowledgeable and experienced in the field of foreign alliances.

Our fighting machine was small and untried. Spain had been a fighting nation for one thousand years; she was ever ready for assaults, rebellions, or defense. Our coastal towns and cities were virtually defenseless. Spain was reputed to have a fleet of 200 warships and 200,000 fighting men, equipped and combat-ready, in Cuba and Puerto Rico. There were many good reasons—far more than exist today—to give the United States official pause in the matter of Cuba.

But on February 15, 1898, a rending blast sank the United States battleship *Maine* in the waters of Havana Harbor and sent 264 American bluejackets to their death. The sinking of the *Maine* while on a peaceful mission in

Spanish waters inflamed the Republic. It provided our young and straining nation with a rallying point and a battle cry. "Remember the *Maine*" galvanized a peaceful nation into war and brought the proud Spanish kingdom to disaster, dismemberment, and loss.

Great provocation, however, does not overnight transform an unprepared nation into a mighty military power capable of waging aggressive war on both land and sea. The job ahead was enormous but it was accepted by a vigorous nation fired to a righteous and indignant patriotism that is too often missing in our land today.

Of course, in those days we could take unilateral action. We could pursue boldly any course dictated by our national conscience without concern over what such action might do to our prestige in an organization such as the United Nations. Nor were we restrained by oversensitiveness to the reaction of other powers to actions we might take. We certainly weren't the most powerful nation on earth at the turn of the century. Nor were we the richest or most influential. But we were, in our convictions and on our willingness to back them, among the most independent of the nations then flourishing. It was this independence— strong, virile, and unafraid—that led us to challenge a much mightier Spain and call her to account for her tyranny over our Western Hemispheric neighbors. It was this independence that led the other nations of the world to treat our fledgling country with the respect due her convictions and her determination.

Now consider our position in the world today. We possess more power, wealth, and influence than any other nation on earth. We have a military capability second to none. We have the productive might to back it up. We have the technology and the resources to do anything—and do it better than any other nation on the face of the globe. We have all these things, but what do they mean in terms of international relations? What do they count for when a Communist-oriented and Communist-directed upstart like Fidel Castro can challenge and insult our flag and all that it stands for? What value has this power and wealth if we are afraid to risk any part of it for our national conscience and the common welfare of the Western Hemisphere?

I would like to quote from a wise old king, King Aratus who lived 220 years before Christ, because I think his words sum up well the attitude of those patriotic Americans who challenged Spanish power in 1898. Here is what Aratus had to say:

"That war is terrible, I grant, but it is not so terrible that we should submit to anything in order to avoid it. Why do we boast of our civic equality and freedom of speech and all that we mean by the word liberty, if nothing is preferable to peace? Peace with justice and honor is the most beautiful and profitable of possessions, but if it is allied with baseness and cowardice nothing is more shameful and disastrous."

As a conservative, I have sometimes been accused of looking backward instead of forward. Perhaps in the case of our relations with Cuba, I should plead guilty to a preoccupation with conditions and attitudes as they existed in the days of President McKinley. I believe they have an important and vital bearing on present-day conditions and actions. I believe that in examining our national attitude, our national interest, and our patriotic temper we do very well to study the past.

Although we were diplomatically geared for unilateral action in the days following the sinking of the *Maine*, we were limited by our immediate capability. We had to mobilize men, money, and ships in greater quantities than ever before in the history of the Republic. And we had to move quickly if we were to protect our defenseless shore-lines from Spanish attack from the sea.

But the nation's spirit, which flared up and flamed as brightly as it had in the days of 1776, was more than equal to the task.

As a first step, Congress—with the unanimous vote of both houses—made immediately available to the President fifty million dollars "for the national defense and for each and every purpose connected therewith." Feverish preparations went ahead for full mobilization of the American people for war.

But the voices of appeasement were not yet quieted. In April of 1898 the diplomatic representatives of Germany, Austria-Hungary, France, Great Britain, Italy, and Russia presented a joint communication to President McKinley expressing the hope that affairs between the United States and Spain could be "amicably adjusted." The President returned a courteous message which, in effect, told the European powers to mind their business and let the United States take care of its own problems. That was on April 7. On April 11 the President sent a message to Congress reviewing the whole sorry situation of the distressed and fettered island of Cuba and declaring that the hour had come for America to act.

The President explained that the rebellion in Cuba was but one in a continuous series of insurrections against

Spain which for more than fifty years had kept the island in disturbance and unrest, and which had threatened the security, comfort, and sovereignty of the United States, while the barbarities of the Spanish government had "shocked the sensibilities and offended the humane sympathies" of the American people. Neutrality, he said, was ruinous to Cuba's prosperity and dangerous to America.

Congress acted quickly in the wake of the President's message and unanimously adopted a joint resolution committing the United States to a policy of armed interference in the affairs of Spain and Cuba.

Thus did a great and responsible nation follow its destiny against the warnings and pressures of the six European powers who did not want the inconvenience of an armed conflict in the Americas at that particular time.

This, I might remind you, was in an era when the United States went its own way, formulated its own foreign policy, and met its own responsibilities in the family of nations. It was before we began to allow the attitudes of other nations to weigh heavily in all of our decisions, before we began to fear the reaction of other nations and other blocs of nations to our conduct of our international relations. It was before we had the United Nations providing a forum for anti-American propaganda in our midst. And it was before we had apologists for foreign ideologies and Red-tinted dictators wielding influence on our newspapers and our Department of State.

This was a time when our patriotic fervor ran strong and undiluted. It was a time of national pride and absolute faith. It was a time ruled by the spirit of freedom and justice that had made this nation a beacon of liberty for the world.

And the accomplishments of the American people in these trying days were in keeping with the spirit of enthusiasm which they brought to even the most distasteful of wartime tasks. At the outbreak of war, we had an army of approximately 25,000 men. It was necessary to increase our military manpower quickly. President McKinley issued a call for volunteers, and the response was immediate and amazing. Although the call was for only 125,000 men, more than 1,000,000 of America's 6,000,000 able-bodied men offered their services.

The response of the American people to the need for money was equally inspired. To support the largely volunteer army of 300,000 men Congress adopted a "War Loan Act" which asked the people to put up two hundred million dollars on which the government agreed to pay an annual interest of 3 percent.

So great was the American people's faith in the strength and resources of their government that purchasers rushed to buy the bonds. The two-hundred-million-dollar war loan was oversubscribed by five times that amount, strengthening the government and increasing the confidence of the nation. This revelation of the vast resources and the internal strength of the United States led the nations of the world to hesitate and to reconsider before giving aid and comfort to the enemies of this vital young Republic. One after another these nations hastened to declare their neutrality in the war over Cuba.

Thus, a display of American determination and strength immediately commanded the respect of the world, the kind of respect that our vacillating and uncertain course in foreign affairs fails to command in the present crucial time in our history.

I will not here attempt to deal with the courageous and inspiring performance of our people in the conduct of that war with Spain over Cuba. I will merely say that spirit and determination overcame tremendous difficulties to win a decisive victory which broke the back of Spanish power in the Western Hemisphere for all time. The way our people met these difficulties will stand forever as an important chapter in the story of a nation's fortitude. I would like to take you through the steaming jungles with Lieutenant Rowan of West Point as he delivered his famous "message to Garcia," to describe the historic sea exploits of Admiral Dewey and his capture of Manila, and to tell again of the courage shown by the United States Marines at Guantanamo and by Arizona's Rough Riders and their Bucky O'Neil as they charged up San Juan Hill. I would like to remind you of the heroism and the accomplishments of America's doctors who overcame the tropical diseases that assailed our troops.

But what I want to emphasize here is that in the days of the Spanish-American War our spirit and patriotism were such that despite the shortcomings of our youth and our unpreparedness we took action. We won a great victory and we liberated a people. It cost us thousands of lives and millions of dollars. We paid in sickness, and in suffering and sorrow. But, as one historian of the times summed it up:

"All priceless things cost something. Civilization has cost something. Christianity cost something. Let us be done with carping. No war in all history, measured in proportion to its magnificent results—if we could but see them— has cost so little as the Spanish War of 1898."

Yes, the Cuban War of 1898 did cost us. The people knew that it would, but in the name of humanity and freedom in the Western·Hemisphere they were ready to meet the price. Our government knew that it would cost us, and that knowledge did not deter it one whit from doing what had to be done.

Now what is our position today? I am suggesting that the issue to be decided is one of freedom or slavery. There are those among us in this nation who cherish the false notion that by accommodating the totalitarian doctrine of communism we can continue the uneasy peace maintained since the end of World War II. There are those among us who, confronted with the ultimate choice, appear to prefer appeasement and piecemeal surrender of the rights and freedoms of man. And, to our undying national shame, there are those among us who would prefer "to crawl on their bellies to Moscow rather than to face the possibility of war."

At best this whole approach aims at sustaining the *status quo*, the uneasy peace, of the Communist War. It gives no thought to the overriding necessity—for the good of all mankind—that we win decisively the current struggle with the Godless forces of international communism.

We do not seem to realize the enormity of the stakes involved in the Cuban situation. It is a situation made to order for the Communists. It gives them a perfect base for launching and sustaining their ideological offensive throughout the Americas. It gives them an island fortress they can arm to the teeth for any military eventuality the future may offer. It gives them a powerful talking point in the world of public opinion so that they may freely say,

"We are so strong that we are able to establish—without challenge—a showcase for international communism on the southern doorstep of the United States."

This is not only a danger to the United States; it is a disgrace and an affront which diminishes the world's respect for us in direct ratio to the length of time we permit the situation to go unchallenged. I suggest that if the American people are concerned about this nation's prestige throughout the world, let them look to Cuba as well as to Laos or Berlin. Let them ask how our commitments to the United Nations balance the extension of slavery and subversion in the Western Hemisphere. Let them ask whether we still adhere in any slightest degree to the spirit of the Monroe Doctrine, or whether we have surrendered all of our national interests to the collective consideration of other powers.

In the Cuban crisis we have moved with an astounding timidity and indecision. We were mesmerized by the intellectual theory of non-intervention while Castro went on shouting insults, confiscating our property, jailing our citizens, and "courting" the deadliest enemy this world has ever known until the moment he admitted he is and always has been a Communist. Our posture before the world has been that of a paralyzed, confused giant only vaguely aware of the danger confronting him—a giant possessed of all the strength necessary to meet the danger but unable to decide to use it.

Is it any wonder that many foreign peoples believe the United States is weaker than the Soviet Union? This ignorant estimate, let me emphasize, is not important for its own sake. Only the vain and incurably sentimental among us will lose sleep simply because foreign peoples are not as impressed by our strength as they should be. The thing to lose sleep over is what these people, having concluded that we are weaker than we are, are likely to do, and that is to join what appears to be the winning side.

By our refusal to act in Cuba, our refusal to act in this important Hemispheric crisis, we are in fact inviting the undecided peoples of the world to accept Russian claims of invincibility and to line up with the enemy bloc in the Communist War. Our enemies, you may be sure, are making great capital of our inability or our unwillingness to recognize the true implications of a Communist bastion off our southern coast. It is long past the time when we should have recognized the Communist conquest of Cuba for what it is—the most important enemy victory of the Communist War, presaging the immediate establishment of a Cuban Soviet Socialistic Republic and pointing to an early establishment of a Latin American Union of Soviet Socialist Republics.

We should act accordingly. We must make it absolutely clear, in the most explicit terms, that Communist governments will not be tolerated in the Western Hemisphere—and that the Castro regime, because it is such a government, will be eliminated. We should make it clear also that we are ready to use our military and economic strength in this defense of freedom.

There came a time when we clearly could have accomplished this, but to our shame we fell down on our word to our Cuban friends and so the attempt failed. Had President Kennedy stuck to his original decision to go through with the invasion as it had been planned, we might well see a free Cuba today or, at least, a Cuba in effective revolt against Castro and communism. During the night of the launching and the invasion, someone urged successfully that the President call off the air and sea support we, out of pure military necessity, had promised. No military commander in his right mind would consider an assault of this nature, requiring as it did an amphibious landing, without air and sea support. We Americans excel in amphibious landings, in placing troops ashore under heavy enemy firepower. What would have been a relatively easy and inexpensive attempt with this support turned into a fiasco, a very shameful one, without it.

It will not serve us to go into the details of this disgraceful failure now; they have been recounted by far more competent writers than I. Nor will it aid us now to pinpoint the member of the Fearful Foursome advising the President on foreign matters who actually changed the President's mind. What we must squeeze from the failure are the lessons.

Certainly the major lesson is that the Commander-in-Chief, the President, should consult with military people before making military decisions and not solely with people who not only are incompetent in their appointed roles but completely unequipped to serve as military advisers. One would have thought that the dreadful results of Roosevelt's military ineptness—his catastrophic demand for "unconditional surrender" and his equally ill-advised decision concerning Berlin—would have served as warnings forever for any of our Presidents faced with the necessity of making decisions of war. Obviously the lesson was not well learned.

While it was a difficult task to find anything positive about the invasion fiasco, I believe the reaction of the people could be classed as one.

After the incident, I detected for the first time—in my mail and in my conversations with people throughout the country—an awakening to the true meaning of the Castro regime. I also recognized a determination and a willingness to do anything that the President should decide was needed to meet this threat.

These people, and I am sure they were typical of most Americans, wanted action. They were encouraged by Mr. Salinger's announcement that the government was considering a full embargo of Cuba and by the President's brave words to a group of American newspapermen which seemed to restate the Monroe Doctrine. They became restive and discouraged at the delay in developing anything like a firm policy toward Castro in the immediate wake of the invasion fiasco, but they were reasonable and patient, recognizing that the situation required caution and planning.

Then came the tractors-for-prisoners negotiations, and the American people were forced to endure the spectacle of our government sanctioning a response to the blackmail demands of a Communist dictator. The world was presented with a picture of the American people scrambling around to dig up the price to pay off a bush-league tyrant on his own terms. It is true that we owe a debt to those Cuban patriots who sought to free their native land and whom we misled and helped so ineffectively. We owe it to them and to all freedom-loving people throughout the world to develop a firm policy which will speak from strength and which will countenance no bowing to Communist demands.

A declaration of intention such as I propose would immediately free us from our blind and unrealistic acceptance of "non-interventionism" for the mere sake of the theory. It would serve notice on the world that we reserve the right to interfere in situations where world freedom, our own security, and the welfare of our neighbors are directly concerned, and that we shall not entrust these concerns solely to the judgment of others. And I might emphasize, such a declaration would go far toward casting the United States in its proper role as the world's leader.

With this beginning I believe that we should use our importance to the economic and political well-being of other American republics to draw their support. Then I think we should proceed with a relevant and complete economic embargo against Cuba and, if necessary, support it by a military blockade. If, however, these instruments should fail, then we should in concert with the other American states take whatever action is needed to dislodge communism from the front yard of the Western Hemisphere.

Such a course of action is what the world should expect from a nation whose blood and sacrifices bought Cuba's first freedom and from a people fully cognizant of the rights and duties devolving upon the guardians of Western civilization.

I believe such a course is mandatory—regardless of what we may risk—if we are to live up to our American heritage as the champions of freedom in a world confronted with a conspiracy of enslavement. Such a course must be undertaken fearlessly, in full knowledge that our stake is not only our national honor but our national survival. We must undertake it in the spirit of good men, determined to prevent the triumph of evil.

FIVE

THE MONROE
DOCTRINE, 1962

WHAT EVER HAPPENED to the Monroe doctrine?

The Cuban fiasco and our indecisive policy in the face of it bring into sharp focus serious questions about our relationship with America south of our national borders. These are questions that must be faced squarely and answered realistically.

First of all, the existence of Cuba as a Kremlin enclave ninety miles off our mainland raises the pertinent and uncomfortable question above: What ever happened to the Monroe Doctrine?

The world was a far different one from ours, politically at least, when President James Monroe outlined to Congress in 1823 the principles that came to be known as the

Monroe Doctrine. There was at that time a growing fear that Spain was preparing to try to recapture her colonies in the Western Hemisphere, a possibility that worried England even more than it did the still relatively young United States. England wanted to make the declaration a joint one, but we made it unilateral. By this Doctrine we announced to the world that we would view with great alarm any attempt of any country outside our Hemisphere to invade any country within it—and, if necessary, we would back up this alarm with military action. We said to the world, in effect: "Stay out! Do not interfere with any of our governments by force or subversion or we, the United States, will intervene on behalf of the beleaguered country."

None deny that this was a powerful force in the shaping of the destiny of the entire Western Hemisphere. But by 1962, some one hundred and thirty years after its birth, the Doctrine has changed its spots. Though some historians believe that the Monroe Doctrine was never completely effective, experts on Latin American affairs point out that today—so far as the letter of the Doctrine is concerned—it has lost not only its effectiveness but its basic characteristics of earlier days. It has become "Pan-Americanized" during the present century.

Woodrow Wilson, who suggested the founding of a Pan-American League of Nations, believed that the right of unilateral intervention within the Hemisphere should be abandoned and the Monroe Doctrine thereby transformed. But the dramatic shift away from the Doctrine began in 1933 at the Montevideo Conference of American States, when the United States agreed to refrain from the use of unilateral armed intervention in the affairs of the Latin

American countries. The same year Sumner Welles, in a memorandum to the President, said that since the Monroe Doctrine was a doctrine of self-defense for the United States, it could also be considered a doctrine of "continental self-defense."

With the approach of World War II, there was an appreciable measure of Hemisphere solidarity that—although not unanimous—lasted until the end of the conflict. And, in 1945, the Act of Chapultepec outlined the main features of a postwar regional security system for the Western Hemisphere which reaffirmed the principle that every attack upon the integrity, inviolability, sovereignty, or political independence of an American state would be considered an act of aggression against all the other American states.

Then, on April 30, 1948, the Charter of the Organization of American States (OAS) was signed in Bogotá and "continentalized" the Monroe Doctrine in the sense that the task of defending the Hemisphere was now shared by all twenty-one member states.

And now we come to the essential question. What has the Organization of American States done to combat the single obvious threat to our freedom?

I fear that the answer is a simple one—until recently, almost nothing. And the recent exclusion, in February of 1962, of Cuba from the OAS has still to be proved effective.

Communist penetration in the Hemisphere has constituted a serious threat for years. Yet the United States has been unable to obtain anything more than words from the OAS. The 1948 Bogotá conference condemned "the political activity of international communism" as a system "tending to suppress political and civil rights and liberties." The Fourth Meeting of Consultation of Foreign Ministers (1951) was called because of the need "for common defense against the aggressive activities of international communism."

The Communists are engaged in intervention in most of the countries of Latin America. Some of their most zealous interventionists have been using Cuba as a base, and Cubans as well as Communists from the entire Soviet world are working determinedly to deprive our Hemisphere's citizens of their rights and properties and to force our neighbors to become satellites of the Communist empire. These activities on the part of Communists and fellow-travelers are as patent violations of both international law and the Monroe Doctrine as were ever perpetrated.

Yet we have not even been able to obtain sanctions, political or economic, against the now blatantly Communist Castro regime through the machinery of the Organization of American States. As late as the middle of December, 1961, only twelve of the Latin American governments had broken relations with Castro's Cuba—the Dominican Republic, Haiti, Costa Rica, El Salvador, Guatemala, Honduras, Nicaragua, Panama, Colombia, Paraguay, Peru, and Venezuela. At the Punta del Este (Uruguay) conference of the OAS in early 1962, Cuba was at least thrown out of the club. But it was a limited objective achieved by the United States. What we really wanted—a collective break in diplomatic and economic relations with Cuba—we did not get.

Faced with this gravest of threats to all of Latin America from a relentless international communism, some say that the letter of the Monroe Doctrine is dead or unworkable. But the spirit remains alive, and we must keep it alive.

The incredible fact that Khrushchev's noisy little hench-man-puppet Castro stands thumbing his nose and jeering at freedom a few minutes' flight south of our southernmost city is merely one of the many facets of the complex situation that confronts us in the Western Hemisphere today. We must combat Communist subversion throughout the Western Hemisphere—within our own borders and throughout South and Central America—with every weapon in our arsenal. We are also faced with organized anti-Americanism—some Communist-inspired and some based on a long tradition of Gringo-hating.

Here, as elsewhere, we must overcome a vacillating, uncertain national objective. For a century, our Latin American policy has been well-intentioned and inept.

With very few exceptions, the Latin American countries have tentatively taken their stand with the non-Communist world in the global conflict between totalitarian tyranny and popular representative government. But uncertainty has recently begun to arise, so far as Latin America's present and future posture is concerned.

The United States government has been trying for thirty years to appease the Latin American countries by whittling down its traditional legal rights to protect the persons and properties of its citizens in Latin America. This appeasement policy, designed to promote the harmony and general welfare of the Western Hemisphere, has resulted in (1) iron-clad treaty agreements against intervention in the domestic affairs or foreign relations of any Latin American country and (2) the "Pan-Americanization" of the Monroe

Doctrine, as we have seen. For a good many years the United States government has not protected the personal and economic rights of its citizens in Latin America.

During Woodrow Wilson's administration, the Mexicans violated with a large measure of impunity both the personal and the property rights of citizens of the United States. In 1938 Mexican officials seized the big oil properties of our citizens, and the government of Bolivia promptly followed suit the very same year. About a decade later, Juan Perón seized American-owned public utilities in Argentina, triggering a widespread epidemic of such seizures.

The most damaging expropriations of the postwar era took place in Bolivia in 1952, involving moderately valuable mining properties, and Cuba in 1959–1960, involving enormously valuable holdings that included sugar and ranch lands, sugar refineries, and public utilities.

Although Communist influence was felt to have been partially responsible for earlier property violations, it was not until the 1950s that this influence was clearly disclosed. It was noted in Bolivia as early as 1952, in Guatemala during the Jacobo Arbenz regime (1952–1954), and in Mexico, though with less damaging results, somewhat earlier. And, of course, in Cuba both before and after the capture of the Cuban government by Fidel Castro and his associates.

Our policy of armed intervention to protect our citizens was sacrificed to the "good-neighbor" concept. This is one of the factors that contributes to our Latin American problem today, illustrating once again how willing our country has been to abdicate its just rights under international law in an effort to buy a measure of good will. And, ironically, those U.S. citizens who were dispossessed in Latin America were often the people who were making large contributions in many areas to the prosperity of the country.

But, except for Cuba, and isolated instances such as the recent grab of the I. T. & T. system in Brazil, expropriation is by and large a thing in the past. What can we do today about Latin America and about combating our chief enemy, communism?

The first answer is the world-wide answer: establish the single national objective of victory over communism. After that, the primary objective of the Latin American policy of the United States should be to make sure that the neighboring republics continue to identify themselves with our country and its allies in the global struggle for national independence and individual freedom and dignity.

Latin America's common people—the masses and the small, though expanding, middle classes—are likely to decide the outcome of this supremely important contest in their part of the Western world. The political and social influence of Latin America's common people has been increasing since the beginning of this century. At present, in all the twenty countries south of the Rio Grande, the people are either on the move or restless. Dictator after dictator has been overthrown within the last decade. By the beginning of 1960, these old-time despots, often allied with the wealthy landlords, mine-owners, and bankers, had been assassinated or driven from power in most of the nations they ruled. By the beginning of 1962, dictators were in control of only four small Latin American countries.

The strongest aspirations of these people include personal liberty, avoidance of the condemnation of the Roman Catholic Church, and a rapid increase in their scanty material possessions—the last of the three probably the most potent factor. Their concept of liberty is very hazy. Most of Latin America's common people have never possessed liberty in anything aproaching full measure. The present danger is that the Communists, who tell the masses that religion is the "opiate of the people," will exterminate their loyalty to their religion and their church before the people realize that the clergy, for the most part, are their most dedicated friends.

Unless the people can be convinced that a rapid modification of the old order which will serve their aspirations can be carried out, it may prove impossible to frustrate and defeat communism in Latin America. The masses may be too unsophisticated to discover the enormous deception now in process, and too many of their leaders may seal their doom by trying to win favors from both groups in the "neutralist" fashion of Southeast Asia and Africa. Somehow, the common people must be persuaded that a free-enterprise democracy will prove the best means of attaining their primary goals, and that the leadership of their church should no longer be considered an obstacle to their progress.

Our aid programs for Latin America should be fashioned with the view toward helping to promote these changes in Latin America. Priority should be accorded both to socially responsible capitalism and to governments that are most dedicated to progress toward truly representative democracy. Prospects for the development of such socially responsible governments and more efficient private businesses in Latin America seem to be a little brighter now than they were a decade or so ago. Its business communities have been deeply disturbed by recent events in Guatemala, Bolivia, and especially Cuba. Both the businessmen and the government of the United States must do all they can to cultivate and assist Latin American businessmen who have the welfare of their countries at heart.

We should not support any program or project whatever without first giving careful attention to its effect on the attitude of the common people toward the private-enterprise system in their country. Official assistance to programs and projects which might cause Latin Americans to turn more resolutely to socialism would probably defeat our efforts to prevent the spread of the global Communist menace in this part of the world. Socialism in Latin America, as in other underdeveloped areas, is likely to lead to communism—largely because of inexperience, weakness, wastefulness, and corruption in public administration.

I suggest no turning back of the clock in Latin America to the days when we were apt to treat the countries south of the border patronizingly as "poor cousins." But we must insist upon Hemispheric unity against the Communist aggressor. If the OAS can bring itself to take a strong and uncompromising stand against the spread of communism no matter in what form it manifests itself, then I will become an ardent backer of that organization. If the OAS needs energetic leadership, then it is obviously up to the United States to provide it. If the OAS refuses to move in a forthright manner against further Communist expansion, then the United States must take unilateral action.

I cannot believe that the Latin American republics would look askance at any vigorous action we took to oppose communism in this hemisphere. And even if they did, what difference does their criticism make when it is clearly a question of our (and their) freedom. Ultimately they must realize that we are fighting their battle as well as our own.

SIX

THE WORLD COURT

IN THE NEXT THREE CHAPTERS I want to discuss three potential dangers which are with us in various strengths, dangers which are not entirely of Communist origin but, nevertheless, if allowed to develop to their fullest, could redound to the advantage of our enemy. These three are the World Court and the continuous efforts to repeal the Connally Amendment; disarmament, or arms control, as the 87th Congress so cutely termed it; and the United Nations.

I must admit at the outset that to argue against these symbols of light and virtue is a lot like arguing against mother love or the family. But I firmly believe that there is a distinct relationship between the three which Americans concerned about their freedom should fully understand. That common denominator is simply this: the world isn't ready for any of them at this moment in history.

I would not argue that the world will never be ready for their virtues, for I am optimistic enough to believe that as we progress toward higher degrees of civilization, better understanding, clearer communications between the peoples of the world, and as the cultural and traditional heritages of peoples tend more to oneness, we can by mutual agreements and understanding begin to look to the settlement of the difficulties that plague our world.

But that time is not now. Because there will unquestionably come up in the coming session or sessions of the United States Senate another effort to repeal the Connally Amendment, more properly termed the Connally Reservation, this danger will be discussed first.

The Connally Amendment states specifically that the United States' acceptance of the World Court's jurisdiction must not be made applicable to disputes where the matters at issue are "essentially within the jurisdiction of the United States, as determined by the United States."

There are soul-wrenching arguments made on behalf of a World Court. The advocates have a wonderful slogan— "World peace through law." It sounds simple and it sounds foolproof. These advocates, reasoning by induction, say, "law through the courts gives peace in each nation; therefore, law administered by a World Court would give peace to all nations."

The mere simplicity of the term "World Court" concerns me because it is easy for people who are accustomed to the law and order as it exists (or is supposed to exist) in our country to become beguiled with the possibilities of extending this protection to all the peoples of the world by a universal tribunal. Easily convinced, they then urge their Senators to repeal the Connally Amendment in order to achieve the utopia. Senators, being not unlike other men in and out of politics, sometimes respond first and think afterwards. I fear that enough may succumb to these well-intended urgings and expose our people to all the uncertainties of a World Court.

What are some of these uncertainties and outright dangers to our way of life? In our country the establishment of internal law developed from the common ideas and concepts by which we lived culturally, socially, and ethically. *There does not exist in the wide world today any such common grounds, and without them even basic common law cannot be written.*

We in the West practice many things in common, even our court procedures have much similarity; but the practices of the entire family of nations across the world vary to the greatest extremes. To suggest today that what is done regarding a certain situation in Ghana is comparable to what is done in the same situation in Illinois is ridiculous. There is a great disparity in language between nations; even our systems of measuring distances and weights vary from country to country. I cannot imagine that we could, by legislative fiat, overcome such complex differences as custom and law while at the same time we cannot arrive at a common method for weighing potatoes or measuring cloth or clocking the speed of vehicles or speaking. I might point out that we have not even been able to arrive at a definition of a word so simple as "aggression" even though we have wrestled with that problem since the birth of the United Nations.

A logician, examining the assumption that a world court would bring peace to all nations, would probably examine the two institutions—a national court and a world court—to see if they possess the same characteristics. I think he would be disappointed.

A national court is a judicial body interpreting legislative law and common law—its writs are enforced by the sovereign power of the state. A world court has neither international legislation nor international common law—its writs are unenforceable except through the normal means by which nations deal with each other, diplomacy.

The United States, led by the late Senator Connally, made a reservation in its dealings with the International Court of Justice by excluding from the jurisdiction of the court disputes that we in America considered purely domestic, our own business and nobody else's. By such a reservation the United States prevents another nation from submitting our tariff policy, our immigration policy, or our currency problems to the World Court for decision, either under a common law which does not yet exist or under ordinances of the United Nations.

When the United Nations Charter was under consideration in San Francisco in 1945, the proposal to establish a World Court—with compulsory jurisdiction over the member states—created a stumbling block which threatened to prevent widespread acceptance of the UN Charter. Ultimately a compromise was reached. The International Court of Justice was to function only in accordance with a so-called "statute," annexed to the Charter and made a part thereof. Though all members of the United Nations were declared to be parties to the statute and might therefore *voluntarily* resort to the Court for settlement of any particular international dispute, no nation is subject to the general compulsory jurisdiction of the Court except to the extent that it may so agree in a formal declaration deposited with the Secretary General of the United Nations.

The United Nations Charter is a multi-partite treaty and had to be submitted to the President and to the Senate for approval and ratification. The prompt consent of the Senate was obtained on July 28, 1945. This consent was based largely upon the representations made by Mr. Stettinius and the State Department that it in no sense constituted a form of World Government and that neither the Senate nor the American people need be concerned that the United Nations or any of its agencies would interfere with the sovereignty of the United States or with the domestic affairs of the American people.

Swept along in a tide of fervent internationalism, the American people—or at least their representatives who came before the committee to testify or sent statements on the bill—seemed overwhelmingly in favor of accepting the jurisdiction of the International Court. Distinguished jurists and lawyers with world-wide reputations urged acceptance. Dozens of highly respected organizations— among them the American Bar Association, the National Education Association, the YWCA, the League of Women Voters—joined the chorus. The relative unanimity of American public opinion was demonstrated on December 18, 1945, when the house of delegates of the American Bar Association, *without a single dissenting vote,* passed a resolution urging the President and the Senate to take appropriate action "at the earliest practicable time."

The Charter was promptly ratified, but delay occurred in taking action with respect to adopting and filing the United States declaration accepting compulsory jurisdiction of the World Court, as provided by Article 36 of the statute. Senator Wayne Morse, in November of 1945, made an effort to secure the passage of a form of declaration. In July of 1946, the Senate Foreign Relations Committee reported on the Morse Resolution.

Only a year after the Senate had almost unanimously ratified the United Nations Charter there were now a number of Senators who had begun to suspect that certain internationalists, both in and out of the United Nations, were laying plans to have the United Nations exercise the powers of a World State, and to transform various of its agencies into instrumentalities of a World Government. These Senators feared an invasion of our exclusive jurisdiction over domestic affairs.

By a substantial majority, 50 to 12, the Senate voted to write into the Morse Resolution the reservation or condition introduced by Senator Tom Connally which provided that this country's acceptance of the jurisdiction of the World Court *"shall not apply to disputes with regard to matters which are essentially within the jurisdiction of the United States, as determined by the United States."*

For ten years the Connally Amendment has protected the individual citizen of the United States against an unwarranted assumption of jurisdiction by the World Court. The late United States Senator Tom Connally had this to say about the attempts to repeal the Connally Amendment:

"My position on the so-called Connally Reservation has

in no way changed since I originally advocated its adoption. You may remember that, at that time, I said in part:

" 'The United States is the object of envy of many nations of the world and many peoples. Our Treasury is most attractive to them. Immigration to our shores is something they dream of. I do not favor and I shall not vote to make it possible for the International Court of Justice to decide whether a question of immigration to our shores is a domestic question or an international question. It is a domestic question, of course; but the Court might contend it is international in character. . . .

" 'Do we want the International Court of Justice to render judgment in a case involving the navigation of the Panama Canal? The Court might say it is an international stream, like the Dardanelles, and problems relative to it are international problems. Such problems are not international.'

"I believe that the repeal of the amendment which reserves to the United States of America the sovereign right to determine what matters are essentially within the domestic jurisdiction of the United States would be most unwise. And I am far from alone in this belief.

"The Texas Bar Association and many other professional organizations and patriotic societies have written to assure me that they remain very strongly opposed to repeal.

"I wish also to express my deep regrets that a matter of such serious importance as the so-called Connally Reservation is being treated as a propaganda device in an attempt to win an international popularity contest."

Keep in mind that the United Nations World Court

is not bound by statute law or common law or precedent and is possessed of almost unlimited authority. Consider what might happen in a criminal case such as that of Caryl Chessman of California if the radical liberals are successful in their efforts to repeal the Connally Amendment.

Russia does not have capital punishment. This may seem incongruous in the face of political executions and mass deportations, but the Russians profess to believe that capital punishment is wrong. If the Connally Amendment is repealed, it is quite possible that the people of Russia or Cuba or Poland—or any other nation—through private or official organizations—could successfully appeal to the World Court to interfere in such a purely domestic situation as the Caryl Chessman case. For propaganda purposes alone, Russia would leap at such a juicy opportunity.

Frank E. Holman, former President of the American Bar Association, has said that "the power of the World Court can be whatever the World Court decides it should be." It is perfectly conceivable that the World Court might go even so far as to declare null and void some sections of the United States Constitution—on the grounds that the U.S. Constitution was in conflict with "international law."

Since 1946, the United Nations has been quite busy— through its commissions and agencies—justifying the good judgment of those members of the Senate who voted for the enactment of the Connally Amendment. Some of these agencies and commissions have frankly confessed their determination to create World Government. Mr. John P. Humphrey, first director of the Commission on Human Rights, publicly disclosed that in its so-called "Bill of Rights" program the Commission was proposing intervention in matters within the domestic jurisdiction of the member states.

Other UN agencies in the years following 1948 were engaged in spawning treaties designed to control and supervise many of our essentially domestic concerns. Among these agencies were the ILO, UNESCO, GATT, ITU, and FAO. They were threatening to meddle with such purely domestic matters as the kind of teaching and textbooks to be adopted in our public school system; matters of social, economic, and labor legislation; matters of health and socialized medicine; and a treaty to establish an international criminal court which would try Americans in a court made up largely of foreign nationals. American citizens could be transported overseas for trial and deprived of the Constitutional safeguards accorded them under the laws of the country.

When the radicals in 1958 began their well-organized attempt to destroy the Connally Amendment, only a very few Americans had any previous understanding of what vital protection was afforded by this piece of legislation. Senator Humphrey and his supporters suggested then and continue to suggest that the United States is endangering the functioning of the World Court and threatening world peace by not surrendering American citizens to this international jurisdiction.

We are told that we should set a "good example." And the clear implication is that only the United States is holding out against "World Peace through World Law." Nothing could be further from the truth.

Mexico reserves "disputes arising from matters that in the opinion of the *Mexican government* are within the jurisdiction of the United States of Mexico." France reserves "disputes relating to matters which are essentially within the national jurisdiction as understood by the *government of the French Republic*." Liberia reserves "any dispute which the Republic of Liberia considers essentially within its domestic jurisdiction." The Union of South Africa reserves "disputes with regards to matters which are essentially within the jurisdiction of the government of the Union of South Africa, *as determined by the government of the Union of South Africa*."

Pakistan reserves, the Republic of Sudan reserves, India reserves, the United Arab Republic reserves, and Australia reserves. Great Britain reserved—and maintained her reservation until the early 1950s, when British policy turned to placating and appeasing Communist China and Communist Russia.

The World Court is now composed of fifteen members or judges, of which only one is a citizen of the United States.

The founders of this Republic fought, and many of them died, to secure for you and for me the personal protection of the United States Constitution and the Bill of Rights.

Those persons—both public and private—who lately urged the repeal of the Connally Amendment were knowingly or unwittingly declaring themselves willing to sacrifice the protection of the Bill of Rights upon the altar of world government.

Consider for a moment the priceless protection of the Bill of Rights.

Article I of the Bill of Rights provides for freedom of

speech, freedom of the press, freedom of assembly, the right to petition, and prohibits the Congress from making laws respecting an establishment of religion.

The UN World Court could deny freedom of speech, of the press, and of assembly, and is not restrained from making laws respecting an establishment of religion.

Article II of the Bill of Rights protects your freedom to keep and bear arms. The World Court, acting in the interests of "international security"—an undefined term— might, very effectively, prohibit the possession of weapons.

Article V says that no person shall be compelled in any criminal case to be witness against himself, nor to be deprived of life, liberty, or property without due process of law.

The World Court may hold its trials in secret at the discretion of the Court. Evidence can be shut off, the court can provide its own experts, and there is no provision for a defense attorney.

Article VI of our Bill of Rights guarantees a speedy trial, a public trial, and a jury trial in the state or district wherein the crime shall have been committed. It provides that the accused is to be confronted with the witnesses against him and that he may subpoena witnesses in his favor.

The World Court makes no provision for trial by jury. The Court may sit and exercise its judgment wherever the Court considers it desirable. There is no requirement that the accused be confronted by his accusers or that the person on trial have the right to subpoena witnesses in his own behalf.

Because we have enjoyed the protection of the Bill of

Rights from the very birth of this nation, most of us take this protection for granted. I would urge every American citizen thoughtfully to reread the Bill of Rights now—and then consider what life would be like for the individual stripped of this protection.

It has always been the policy of the United States to make every possible effort to settle disputes by peaceable means. Since the beginning of our Republic we have solved disputes of national and international character by voluntary arbitration. But we have never surrendered interpretation and enforcement to compulsory adjudication by a World Court. I hope that we never do.

Too often in this country we have been trapped—in our idealism—by the clever use of slogans. "World Peace through Law" is a good example. It is an old trick to say "Are you for world peace?" "Are you for law?" Naturally we all want peace and we believe in law.

But do the Communists? And do the words "peace" and "law" mean to them what they do to us? The answer to both questions must be an emphatic *"No!"*

I would not want to leave in the reader's mind the impression that there is *never* going to be any future for a tribunal such as an international court. The entire world hopes there will be, and in truth should be working toward that day. But to attempt to make it work at this period in our history would bring disaster, not understanding. It may be decades, it may be hundreds or even thousands of years before the world reaches a cultural, social, and economic level which will develop the conditions under which a central or world type of court can operate, but it has not arrived at that place as of now.

This does not mean that we as people should not concern ourselves with the problems others face. It is a challenge to those of us who have reached a higher plateau of civilization and are going still higher to help those who have not. This will be done only by example and by teaching and by patience, keeping ever in mind the long struggle which our forebears endured to get us where we are. The going will be slow and the way will be hard.

But when, you ask, will mankind have advanced to the point where such an all-powerful international court will be practical? I am a superficial student of history at best, but let me refer you to words of one of the world's great historians, Arnold Toynbee, who suggests that progress toward utopia is slow indeed:

"If you want to understand the Sumerians in 3000 B.C., Kennedy and Khrushchev help bring them alive. I think human nature and the ways human beings deal with each other are the same as they have always been, at least as far back as records allow us to judge."

SEVEN

DISARMAMENT

THE IDEA OF DISARMAMENT is a beautiful one. No man can deny that. In practical realistic terms, however, at this moment in history, the disarmament concept is an effective weapon in the hands of the Communists and a danger to the freedom of mankind.

I suppose that ever since man has resorted to armaments other than his fists, he has dreamed about and talked about each side throwing down its weapons so that the danger of conflict would be banished forever. Now if the disagreements and misunderstandings that make armaments necessary could be discovered and removed, then we could discuss removing the arms. But as long as people have a basic loyalty to their own country's aims and policies and their own way of life, those people will be necessarily concerned with the retention of those things and will fight for them with any and all weapons they can put their hands on.

If I might use the old "tail wags dog" analogy, this basic understanding between peoples is the dog and disarmament is the tail that must follow. But right now the proponents of disarmament, years ahead of themselves, are making the tail wag the dog.

I don't propose to go back through the history of the failure of these disarmament proposals. Rather I will confine myself to discussing some obvious reasons why they will not work in the world today as they have not worked in the world of yesterday. The reasons never change. In doing this, I hope that we can recognize the advantage which has accrued to the Soviet thus far in these phony disarmament talks. It is another lesson that will serve us well as we proceed in the winning of this Communist War.

Often, in speaking about the current efforts of Khrushchev to entice us into tricky disarmament discussions, I have likened Russia to a giant of a man, maybe six feet ten inches tall, weighing 275 pounds, trim and hard as nails, who with one swipe of his hand could render me "hors de combat." But this giant never bothered me because I had in my possession a pistol which he knew I would use as an "equalizer" if he made one threatening move toward me. This worked fine but one day he turned to me and said, "Goldwater, let's you and I talk disarmament."

Now who would be expected to do the disarming? I would, of course; and the moment I yielded to this silly demand, I would be at his mercy. Put Russia in the giant's place and the Western Powers in mine and the hypothetical situation—though a crude one, I admit—begins to make a little sense. Russia with her land mass and her large and well-equipped ground and sea forces has been held in check by our "equalizer," which is overwhelming air power and the nuclear bomb. What would be the subject of disarmament talks? Why, air power to be sure, because ground and sea power are historical in their dimensions and we just do not discuss traditional weapons in such meetings. And the moment we began to yield on air power, we would be placing ourselves in a position of irreparable weakness.

What the Communists are designing was well and colorfully illustrated by, I believe, Winston Churchill. Later Salvador de Madariaga used the idea in his excellent book on the Communist War, *The Blowing Up of the Parthenon, or How to Lose the Cold War.* It goes like this: "The animals decided to disarm, and held a conference for that purpose. The eagle, with an eye on the bull, suggested that all horns should be razed off. The bull, with a squint at the tiger, thought that all claws should be cut short. The tiger, glaring at the elephant, was of the opinion that tusks should be pulled out, or at any rate shortened. The elephant, staring at the eagle, thought it indispensable that all wings should be clipped. Whereupon the bear, with a circular glance at all his brethern, cried out: 'Why all those half-way measures? Let all weapons be done away with, so that nothing remains in the way of a fraternal, all-embracing hug.' "

The United States could very well be any of those animals except the bear, for during the past six years we have been pulled into an almost endless conference where, if we had followed the insistence of the Communists, we could have found ourselves in the position of having done away with our weapons of strength, aiding the "fraternal, all-embracing hug" of our enemy, the Soviet bear.

In these conferences, the complexity of disarmament grows as the Soviet representatives want it to. Their purpose is to becloud the basic issues which make arms a necessary evil. They confuse us while they tempt us. In a fine new book by Strausz-Hupe, Kintner, and Possony, *A Forward Strategy for America,* an excellent sequel to *Protracted Conflict,* the authors provide an exhaustive list of the many subjects which have been proposed for negotiation since 1955. These bewildering proposals break down as follows: (a) geographical zones of disengagement, e.g., Central Europe; (b) the establishment of nuclear-free zones, e.g., Central Europe, Antarctica, and the Western Pacific; (c) the exercise of self-restraint among the major powers in the shipment of arms to troubled spots, e.g., the Middle East, Africa, or the Caribbean; (d) reduction in the size of conventional armed forces among the major powers; (e) special control arrangements for nuclear weapons, e.g., a ban on tests and on the production of fissionable materials for military purposes, the reduction or elimination of existing nuclear weapons stockpiles, a ban on the production of weapons devices or control of the number produced, elimination or control of the means of intercontinental delivery; (f) the elimination of great-power bases on foreign territory; (g) control of the passage of military craft on, under, or over, the oceans of the world; (h) control of outer space, especially a prohibition against orbiting weapons of mass destruction and against the laying of national claims to any extraterrestrial body or area of outer space, in order to prevent the erection of spheres of armed influence; (i) prohibiting the testing, production, and use of chemical and bacteriological weapons; (j) control of the means of irregular warfare—guerrilla forces, paramilitary organizations, and other international subversive agencies; and (k) safeguards against surprise attack, as well as nuclear war by technical accident, human error, or political miscalculation, e.g., provocation with unanticipated results, limited war followed by "escalation" or "catalytic war."

These complications are but the beginning of our troubles. Experience in countless conferences with the enemy has shown us that they do not want these meetings to end, and when a terminal situation develops, they shift their emphasis to another area related in just enough of a way to entice us to continue. They are masters at this type of protracted intrigue. The experiences of those unfortunates in American business who have had to negotiate with Communist-controlled unions in this country can relate a similar experience of talk and more talk, attack and retreat, suggest and counter-suggest aimed only at prolonging the talks and wearing down the patience and good sense of the man across the table.

Nations do not arm for war. They arm to keep themselves from war. No nation in its right mind ever uses war except as the last instrument available for the achievement of its objectives and policies. And, believe me, our enemies are nations in their right minds. They know what they want and they have been achieving many of their desires without war. They will resort to war only, in my opinion , when one of two conditions prevails: (1) If there is a decisive switch in world affairs to the point where it is obvious they are going to lose, or (2) if we continue to appease and accommodate them, and disarming would certainly be in this category.

When we discuss this subject we are not confining ourselves to Russia and the United States. We must talk about all nations, particularly when we bring up the subject of nuclear weapons. In this field, for example, France and Red China have not even been a party to the Geneva disarmament negotiations and both have very serious intentions relative to nuclear development.

When we begin to talk seriously of world-wide disarmament and the procedures, the mechanics, the methods of accomplishing it, the path becomes a maze no man or country could follow without great difficulty. Most thinking people agree at the outset that total disarmament can never be achieved because of the need inside each country for enough weapons to maintain local order and control lawless elements. So it becomes, even at the start, a question of *partial* disaramament. And here further complications set in. If, for instance, the decision were reached to halve the world's armaments, how would we develop an arrangement that was equitable all around? We cannot assume that we would all start from the same position. Some are stronger than others and some are pitifully weak. Halving would leave the strong strong when compared to the weak, who would only be made weaker. But let us bypass this problem. In this hypothetical case of halving, how would we go about it? Would we abolish bombers but retain fighter craft because in the case of local revolution they could be useful? (Fighters also carry most kinds of bombs and rockets.) Would we abolish the submarine and retain light carriers? (Planes from light carriers can drop bombs.) Would we abolish the warhead but retain the bomb? (Bombs can have important peacetime uses, such as the creation of harbors.)

If, on the other hand, the approach were to allow each country to retain weapons in ratio to its population, we would be faced with the ridiculous situation of China and India in a mad arms race to catch up with their population —while the highly developed countries of the West would be throwing their arms away.

Now suppose that the nations of the world, sitting around a conference table, agreed to eliminate the atomic and nuclear bombs altogether for wartime use as weapons but approved of the fission process for peaceful uses. Two problems would face us. The country having the largest number of soldiers (Russia or Red China) would have the largest inventory of conventional weapons, so we in the West would be at an immediate disadvantage. The second problem is the old one of inspection: who will see to it that some peacefully intended use of the fission process is not clandestinely turned into a monstrous weapon to be used just once to begin and end a war?

Now the mere fact of the existence of nuclear weapons does not make disarmament an imperative policy. I do not subscribe to the theory that nuclear weapons have changed everything—that we must now have complete disarmament or the world will go up in flames. And even if I did subscribe to such a theory, how would I or anyone else ever be assured that our enemy in the Communist War would adopt a similar attitude? Certainly, the Russians will not adopt any kind of disarmament so long as revolt lies seething just below the surface in their satellite nations. We have in the nuclear bomb an advance in weaponry, and terrible though that advance is, it still is merely a more efficient means of destruction. In a historical and relative sense, it can be compared with the advance made in military operations by the invention and adaptation of gunpower to war-making and the development of aerial warfare and strategic bombing missions.

The only real disarmament will come when the cause for arms is removed. In our case that cause is communism. In the Soviets' case, that cause is the free world. Does anyone believe that they will voluntarily give up their gains and their objectives? Does anyone believe that we will give up our way of life and settle for peace under slavery? Those few among us who, because of a paralyzing fear of death itself, would rather be "red than dead" need a lesson in history. The idea of freedom cannot be stamped out by the scratch of a pen. Patrick Henry said it in a few ringing words two hundred years ago, and his "Give me liberty or give me death" rings just as true today.

On the other side of the coin, the ideas of power and control of people and their lives are not going to be discarded easily by the rulers of communism, to be traded for the ideologies of free men. Especially is this true because Communists have, with the use of relatively few weapons, gained control over one-third of the people of this earth and already foresee the day when universal and complete success will be theirs. Ideas are what we are talking about, and ideas are not materially destroyed as we would destroy a piece of paper or a car or a house. They are replaced by other ideas—sometimes by better ideas and sometimes by worse. Our job is to prove and sell our set of ideas—not to destroy by disarmament the means we have of protecting them if that becomes necessary.

History teaches us that armament races are no more than a symptom of international friction, not a cause of it. Unless the basic disagreement between the Western world and communism can be resolved, any suggestion of disarmament is illusory and deceptive.

The Communists are dedicated to the destruction of the Western world, by peaceful means if possible, by war if necessary. We cannot by dropping our guard, by diminishing our ability to defend ourselves, create a situation conducive to world peace. In fact, it is probable that any disarmament by the Western world would be construed by the Russians as a sign of weakness and an invitation to a Communist thrust.

The Communist leaders may preach general disarmament for propaganda purposes. They may also seriously promote mutual disarmament in certain weapon categories in the knowledge that their superior strength in other weapons would leave them, on balance, decisively stronger than the West. Thus, in the light of the West's comparative weakness in conventional weapons, it might make sense for the Communists to seek disarmament in the nuclear field. If all nuclear weapons suddenly ceased to exist, much of the world would immediately be laid open to conquest by the masses of Russian and Chinese men under conventional arms.

We should, I believe, announce in no uncertain terms that we are *against* disarmament. We are against it because we *need* our armaments—all of those we presently have, and more. We need weapons for both the limited and the unlimited war.

I do not suggest that any of our responsible leaders take disarmament seriously at this time. They certainly do not favor unilateral disarmament, and they know the Soviets are not going to join us in any mutual disarmament that is not to their advantage. What I object to is saying we favor disarmament. The danger here is that we become hoisted by the petard of our own propaganda.

This has already happened in the critical matter of nuclear tests—so vital to our national security. We originally agreed to suspend our tests, partly on the misguided notion that the Russians were seriously interested in devising an adequate system of inspection and controls. But mostly we were feeling the pressure of a "world opinion" we helped create concerning the dangers of radioactive fallout and the ultimate horrors of a nuclear holocaust. Now that the illusions about Soviet intentions have been dispelled by their 50-megaton bomb, and though the danger of fallout from the kind of underground and stratospheric testing we propose is nonexistent, we *still* find it difficult to resume testing for fear of offending the brooding, finger-pointing ghost of world opinion.

It is difficult, I admit, for us to match and counteract Soviet propaganda concerning the desirability of general disarmament. Once again strong world pressures are bearing down upon us to "do something" about it. And Western leaders, unlike the men in the Kremlin, characteristically find such pressures difficult to resist.

The function of our counter-propaganda should be to educate the people of the world about the realities of life

—not to promote an escape from them. Plain talking on the subject of disarmament is necessary. A lucid analysis of the hypocrisies of the Soviet position must be conveyed to the thinking people of the world again and again and again.

There is a possibility which exists in two forms which just might become the catalytic agent in developing a system for the control of the use of arms and lead eventually to possible disarmament. General Eisenhower when‘he was President said that disarmament could only come about with a foolproof and completely dependable system of inspection. In other words, every nation of the world would have to have constant access to the military weapons inventory and disposition of every other nation. Since 1960, General Eisenhower has reiterated and expanded this idea with me in private talks.

I believe that any rational thinker on this subject would have to agree with this wise and basic assumption. Of course, we have no indication that Russia has any intentions of allowing herself to be regularly inspected by any other nation. Thus General Eisenhower's suggestion becomes at once an impossibility if it is to be approached in the manner in which we usually think of "inspection."

Let us remember, however, that because of a dangerous lack of information relative to the Soviet military capabilities, particularly in the fields of missiles and rockets, it became necessary for us to institute the famous U-2 flights. The sole purpose of those flights was to accomplish what a tight security system in Russia prevented our accomplishing in the usual way, the gathering of military intelligence.

Now let us extend this idea, first one step and then another. The machinery for accomplishing the first step is almost at hand, but the needed vehicles for the second, while already at work, need perfecting, and that will take more time. The B-70, reconnaissance version, can be in the air by the end of 1962 if the administration does not drag its feet on production. This is an aircraft capable of at least two thousand miles an hour at altitudes of at least eighty thousand feet. A sufficient number of these to guarantee a complete photographic record of the entire world, country by country, every day, such photographs to be made available to every nation as soon as they have been processed, would give the world needed military intelligence to point the finger of public opinion at any offending nation. Here we could put to work for the interest of peace the very weapon Russia has been using so effectively against peace; namely, world opinion.

The B-70 project could be financed by the United States alone or in concert with other nations able to afford it, but the information would become the property of the entire world. This means of obtaining information would continue until—and here is step number two—we have perfected the art of satellite reconnaissance to such a degree that it can be depended on for sharp, accurate pictures of the entire earth's surface. This would include the ability constantly to transmit these pictures so that all countries could receive them. Again, the wealthier nations could provide the monies for this effort, but all countries would benefit.

If these pictures showed the undue movement of troops or equipment, or the erection of new missile bases or new factories for the manufacturing of war equipment, the world would immediately know of it and the force of world public opinion could be brought forcefully to bear. If this world public opinion could be crystalized into an intelligent expression of feeling, we might see developing a world commonwealth really concerned with peace and able to do something about it. It would not be a highly centralized bureaucratic world government. But based on the concept that the people of the world always want peace and will only abandon this attitude when their own lives or way of life are threatened or when they are tricked into action by selfish power-minded rulers, this commonwealth I speak of would confine itself to the pursuit of peace and the avoidance of war.

If any country resented this method of inspection and set about to destroy the aircraft or the satellite, the world would immediately know who wants peace and who does not. An action such as this would galvanize the world into taking steps against the known aggressor and, realizing this, it is doubtful that any country would deliberately bring down an aircraft or destroy the functioning of a satellite engaged in this assignment for peace.

One technological advance looms larger than any other at this time. That is the progress the world has made in communication. No longer does it take months to get word from the interior jungles of Africa to the outside. It goes out as it is happening. As means of communicating around the world become even faster, it will become easier and easier to provide the peoples of the world with immediate information on which to form their opinions and act. Just as it is now possible within the boundaries of one country to crystallize opinion, it will become possible to do it on a global basis. Peace being the desire of all, the people of the world will not look kindly on any one nation or group of nations who, by their instantly revealed actions, are taking steps to destroy peace.

I am not suggesting that we continue desperately to seek the good will of all people. Nor do I suggest that other people change their ways to impress us favorably. What I am talking about is harnessing world opinion quickly and directing it at an obviously power-mad nation or group of nations.

Today we can talk until we are blue in the face about the aggressive attitude of the Communists and their build-up of arms with little effect on world opinion. But talking about it and seeing it are two different things. The Communists, for example, speak of peace. They seem to be offering complete disarmament in four years. But then they speak in the next breath of burying us and our children growing up under communism. It is next to impossible to get people to understand that they speak of peace as war and war as peace, and that they will only be happy when they dominate the world and freedom has vanished.

But under this system of constant observation and immediate communication, perhaps the Communists could be made to put up or shut up. It is a plan worthy of our most serious consideration.

EIGHT

THE UNITED NATIONS

IT WAS GEORGE WASHINGTON, an early American opponent of entangling alliances with foreign powers, who admonished the American people to "be friendly but keep your hedges high."

Until the end of World War I our people as a whole continued to feel no acute political or economic responsibility to those who lived outside the borders of the United States.

Even at the time we were entering into that war we felt it necessary to make the distinction, through our President, that our efforts in aid of the British and French against Germany were less those of an allied power than those of a contributor to the effort to defeat the mutual enemy. At the end of the war, President Wilson made the first American effort to bring this country into close alliance with

127

other nations by strongly urging that we become a part of the newly formed League of Nations, but the strong feeling for resisting such compacts, carried throughout our nation's history, prevailed and we refused to become a party to the League.

As World War II began to draw to a close and the results were becoming obvious to the world, another United States President, Franklin Roosevelt, with his inordinate skill as a political maneuverer, drummed up not merely enthusiastic and optimistic support for the new idea, the United Nations, but enough power to see the Wilsonian idea from the First World War translated into being at the end of the Second World War. The anti-alliance feeling, described as isolationism and held by an overwhelming number of Americans, was overnight made unpopular. In fact, one who spoke in the American prewar vein found himself about as acceptable in this society as the Piltdown man.

We have lived now over fifteen years not only as a participating member of the United Nations but as its fairy godfather, who although he foots nearly half the bills yet has no more effect in its councils than the enemy of free men, or the smallest and the newest of nations. It is only natural, then, that Americans now are looking at this child of World War II and are asking polite and pertinent and very timely questions about it. What does it do for the furtherance of freedom in the world? What will be the effects of its actions or non-actions on freedom and on our own national objectives? Were we right in the days before World War II in holding that we should avoid entangling alliances with foreign powers? These and many other questions are in the minds of Americans today as we watch a world still in turmoil after these years devoted to working within the UN for mutual solution of world-wide problems.

It is not strange, then, to hear again in our country expressions of what we must identify as a form of isolationism. I do not feel that this movement will bring about a return to the accepted prewar meaning of the term; in fact, we must work to prevent that. But we can only prevent it from happening by some clear and honest interpretations of what has taken place in the tall, slab-like building in New York City. Americans have a great capacity for going to extremes. In our era we will demonstrate this if we do not hold the United Nations in proper perspective.

Running counter to this growing tide of isolationism is the equally disturbing one of internationalism, a movement already more extreme than its counterpart. It is among the internationalists, of course, that we find the most vociferous of the UN backers. These people believe in a "world government now." They see in the United Nations "the only hope of the world," "the only wall between total nuclear war and us." They are as brainwashed as those who say we must stand alone on our shores and defy the world. Avoiding these two extremes, we must diligently pursue all courses that might produce some answers to serve the true interests of freedom. I say freedom, not peace, because peace without freedom is unacceptable to the American people.

Let me revert to my contention that there is a meeting ground between those who believe this nation can best serve its own interests and the interests of the free world by working as a lone agent concerned first, last, and always with our objective, the extension of freedom, and those who see our position as one embracing and trying to solve the economic, political, and social problems of every other nation in the world. We cannot hold today that we can isolate ourselves from the rest of the world. What happens in Ghana, or Vietnam, or in Cuba has a direct bearing on American security. Nor can we, also to maintain our security, be completely internationalist. World government is certainly not something we should be advocating at the present time.

The meeting ground may be found in a new form of nationalism extremely sensitive to our responsibilities to ourselves and to our own objectives, and at the same time cognizant that the ability of other free nations to resist the Communist thrusts is a matter of concern to Americans. A recognition by the President himself that victory over the Communists is a national goal—held by all Americans to be in the vital interest of the country and the free world—would be the keystone of this new nationalism. Once we have come to this, I firmly believe that the extremes will largely disappear. With a common purpose, Americans and the free peoples will begin to make a world in which communism will play a decreasingly important role and freedom will emerge as the guiding force of destiny.

This new nationalism, searching as it must for areas of agreement between the friendly nations of the free world, must avoid complete reliance on any organization whose total interest does not coincide with freedom. The United Nations is one of these. The politically powerful clique in our midst which looks not at what the UN accomplishes, but only listens to what it promises, will not agree that there are inherent weaknesses in a group such as the UN. In agreement with this clique will be found a large segment of the press, some professors, the big foundation executives, and quasi-political associations, all of whom exercise a considerable influence over public opinion in this country. It will not be easy to overcome this influential advantage, but through continuing and honest evaluation of what the United Nations does and does not do for the cause of freedom, we can judge the need for a new nationalist position and the need for a United Nations as it is now set up. The UN now is quite a different organization from the original conception of what it would be. I venture to say that had its originators told the Senate of the United States what their baby would grow into within fifteen years, the Senate would have voted no on the proposition that we join it.

Originally, it was to be an open forum for disputes between nations, where arguments could be settled by compromise in a way that would be acceptable to most, if not all, of the members. It was never intended that its will be imposed upon an unwilling member; in fact, without a military force ready at all times, this would in itself be an impossibility, as has been discovered. Even to imagine a powerful military force (not the meager police force the UN has now) being conscripted from such a hodgepodge of nations—mature and immature, economically strong and dangerously weak, divided in allegiance and obviously distrustful of one another—would tax the powers of the most gullible and naïve. The UN has rejected opportunities to arbitrate. In Kashmir, for instance, it refused to do so because Nehru, the paragon of virtue when the actions of democratic countries are in question, refused to allow such a course and, in fact, prevented it with arms. When faced with opportunities to make its decisions effective by a show of arms, the UN has placed the responsibility on a few, the largest load invariably falling on the United States.

At the outset we failed to recognize the true intents of the Communists in and out of the UN. We saw them as ex-comrades in arms and as brethren of the peace who would sit around the conference table in a true spirit of give-and-take, helping solve the problems of the world. We have found since, to the world's regret, that their intransigence has made impossible of achievement most of the UN's original goals.

We have found, also, that the new nations with their understandable political naïveté come in either as uncommitted (neutral) nations or leaning toward the Soviets because, in their opinion, the Soviets dominate the Council through their incessant use of the veto and their strength in the General Assembly. We felt we would always have sufficient votes there to safeguard the interests of freedom. We now find that majority being whittled down to a point where if the abstaining votes in the poll of 1961 on the admission of Red China had been cast for her entry, we would have suffered a major defeat.

The United Nations has changed internally because of Communist pressure. We have no reason to expect any magical change for the better. Politically powerful Americans pay no attention to *results*, and the Communists pay unwavering attention to results, particularly those directly beneficial to them. We have seen the inexplicable and disgusting episode in the Congo when the United Nations, financed by forty million dollars of U.S. money, brought war into Katanga, the one part of the Congo where there was peace and a growing prosperity, and insisted that the government there submit to a Communist-dominated central authority.

We are members of the United Nations and, for going along with these senseless procedures, we are as guilty as the rest. This is why I suggest that we must not depend blindly on the UN for the spreading of freedom. It has a value as a forum before which the various nations may vent their pleasure, their spleen, or their problems. We should stay with the forum so long as the actions of the UN do not violate our national objective and do not continue to serve the Communists as they have in the past.

On past occasions, when we have subordinated to United Nations policy our own notions of how to wage the Communist War effectively, Western interests have suffered. The Korean War, the Suez crisis, the Iraqi Revolution, this year's events in the Congo, all demonstrate this. This experience should not surprise us when we remember that United Nations policy has been the common denominator of the foreign policies of eighty-odd nations, some violently hostile to us, some indifferent to our interests, nearly all less determined than we to save the world from Communist domination. In the future, with the growing influx of allegedly neutral nations from Asia and Africa, continued American deference to Soviet Russia will invite dire consequences.

The important development at the UN has not been what communism has done with its right hand—Khrushchev's shoe-banging display and his name-calling, for instance—but what communism has accomplished with its left—the successful campaign to get the current Soviet foreign-policy line endorsed by a bloc of allegedly neutral nations. Messrs. Tito, Nkrumah, Sukarno, Nehru, and Nasser—although their proposals have been pro-Soviet in every particular—became a kind of phony "centerist" bloc whose favor we found ourselves earnestly courting. This was a bizarre indication that the power center of the United Nations had moved sharply to the left. And there have been others: the resolution against nuclear testing, the resolution calling for the immediate end of all colonialism, the connivance of the United Nations in Lumumba's temporary return to power.

We must liberate ourselves and other people from the superstition that international policies to be "good" policies must have the approval of the United Nations. This is a part of liberating ourselves from the confining clutches of world opinion.

There may be occasions when the United Nations can be utilized to provide a broad base of agreement to policies that further Western interests. But when submission of a matter to the United Nations predictably will obstruct the pursuit of American policy, then we must, as we did in the case of Berlin, quietly insist on settling the problem elsewhere.

Concerning this question of the virtue of supporting the UN, it may be useful to quote the very perceptive comments of the Catholic bishops of the United States in their statement of November 20, 1960:

The tendency "to delegate excessive responsibility to an organization is discernible also in the realm of international affairs. Some manifest no sense of personal responsibility in the affairs of the international community. On the other hand, many citizens seem to feel that our mere adherence to the United Nations absolves us from further responsibility in the international order and that decisions made by the United Nations, regardless of their objective value, are always to be regarded as morally right.

"Admitting the undoubted value of a policy of supporting the United Nations and recognizing the genuine contribution it has made in many areas, we must understand clearly that the citizens of this country, and of all countries, have a responsibility to judge and to evaluate the United Nations' deliberations and decisions according to objective norms of morality universally binding. This involves also the duty of citizens to make proper representations of such judgment to their respective governments."

This last sentence provides a real key to getting the United Nations into proper perspective. The responsibility for conducting the foreign affairs of our nation is placed in the hands of the Executive Branch of government acting with the advice and consent of the Senate. One-third of that body is subject to the approval or disapproval of the people every two years, and if the representations of the citizens have not been heeded, then the ballot box expresses their views.

If we recognize, as it has become evident we must, that the common interests of the free world are to be found in alliances outside the UN and that the "free world" means those countries sharing a common interest in freedom and against communism, then finding those countries does not pose a great problem. We already have alliances with the

North Atlantic countries, the Latin countries, and the Southeast Asian countries. With all of these we have much in common. We share a desire for freedom. To a greater or lesser degree we have economic systems operated by the determinations of the marketplace. We share also, to a varying degree, the knowledge that communism is our enemy.

To point up what I mean by "varying degree," the Argentine army is conducting an anti-guerrilla school, but contrary to our similar school in Panama, which stresses tactics first, theirs stresses a study of Communist doctrine, its history and its application. The leader of the school makes this very interesting statement. "We have not only to fight the Communists, we have got to fight communism. To do this, we have to understand it thoroughly." (In the United States we not only do not stress the need for this knowledge in our own guerrilla school, but by top-level civilian edict we discourage the teaching of it anyplace in our armed services.)

Regardless of certain areas of disagreement, these groups of nations within these alliances have more compatibility than lack of it, and the fact that we are the prime targets of the Communists binds us to a joint objective: victory over that philosophy and the furtherance of ours in the world. If we can strengthen our positions politically and economically, not only individually but as a group of free nations, we will be in a position effectively to stem the progress of communism. We have failed to exploit the propaganda advantages of Western powers' economic growth in Europe versus the lesser improvements in Russia and the downhill slide in the satellite countries. Almost on Russia's doorstep lies the area (Europe) showing the clearest distinction between the free world and the slave world. Yet we have allowed the Communists to focus world interest on faraway places and turn attention away from this disadvantageous comparison. It is by no means too late to show this economic gap, and the difference between free and slave states will continue to grow as long as the powers of Europe continue to foster free enterprise in the varying ways in which they do.

The powers embraced by NATO, SEATO, and OAS can form the great dam against the running tide of communism, for we will find in these alliances industrially strong countries who can aid those who have not yet reached the same high plateau. The greatest work we can do for our neighbors in the Latin American countries is to extend to them the technical knowledge we were required to gain so that our lands would produce and our natural resources would become sources of wealth and well-being for all the people. The Latin American countries will have a population, by the year 2000, of over five hundred million people. To cement the friendship between the peoples of this Hemisphere, we will have to strengthen their resistance to communism.

We can give to the people of Southeast Asia the strong hand of assistance when they are attacked, and the equally strong hand of our technical knowledge in peacetime, so that they can get from their lands, their resources, and their toil the benefits we have from ours.

There are many other countries rising from the deserts and the jungles of the world. These new nations cannot be left outside the orbit of the friendship of the established nations of the free world. We must, however, look at their problems in a realistic way. Take, for example, those nations emerging on the great continent of Africa. We must remember our own early attempts to create a government, and the long years of argument and indecision. We must recognize the difficult but necessary task of elevating these nations culturally, economically, and politically to the point where they are capable of responsible self-government. We cannot leave them to the Communists. At the same time we must convince them that we have no "colonial" designs.

It may be that native leaders will emerge friendly to the West who, with our support, can lead their people to some measure of orderly, progressive self-government. Perhaps Colonel Mobutu is such a leader, but probably we shall never know. For in the eight weeks in which Western fortunes in Africa rested on his shoulders, we seem not to have lifted a finger to help him. Today, events in the Congo, with the active cooperation of the United Nations, are helping to consolidate in power a "neutralist" government whose sympathies, I predict, will become more and more pro-Communist.

Where such leaders have not emerged, the West must remain involved. We cannot acquiesce in independence movements where independence means Communist domination or a return to savagery. Nor can we afford to jump on the bandwagon of anti-colonialism and so accelerate the mad rush toward anarchy and Soviet peonage. In areas where Western power still prevails, the full weight of American diplomacy must be employed to sustain it. In areas that have already fallen under Communist influence, we must proceed, overtly and covertly, to restore Western influence.

Perhaps the answer is an interim African Protectorate administered by an association of Western nations. The purpose of such a protectorate would be to preside over a crash program preparing the African people economically, politically, and culturally for the responsibilities of self-government in an atmosphere conducive to the triumph of Western concepts of justice and freedom. Such a policy would be denounced in many parts of the world as reactionary, chauvinistic, and oppressive. Such recriminations we would have to endure. For there would be no doubt in our minds that the colonial system, even in its present state of development, is better for the African people than the misery and chaos into which they are now plunging headlong.

We would hold on to Africa, in part because Western survival there is essential to victory over communism, but no less because we know that the privilege of being born in the West carries with it the responsibility of extending our good fortune to others. We are the bearers of Western civilization, the most noble product of the heart and mind of man. If, in Africa, the West has failed in the past to do the full measure of its duty, then all the more reason for doing our duty now.

In summation then, the United Nations will not be a danger to the achievement of our objectives if we keep it in its proper place and do not allow it to become a sort of summit beyond which there can be no appeal. To avoid this will not be easy because of the powerful forces at work dedicated to the idea of the organization and without sense of its failures and its limitations. These people, I suggest, are the core of the group who saw no harm in admitting to the UN Outer Mongolia, which sent five thousand men to help the Communists in Korea. This is the group that would admit Red China, which exists today only because of this same group's refusal to allow victory over the Red Chinese in the Korean War.

The threat that Red China will be made part of the United Nations is so strong that I will deal with it separately in the following chapter.

NINE

RED CHINA
AND THE UN

IN THE AFFAIRS of nations, the time to take strong action inevitably comes. Such a time is with us now almost constantly. The Communists are moving on many fronts, among them the United Nations.

One of Communist strategies to undermine our position in the Far East is to insinuate Red China into the United Nations. Each year supporters of that maneuver tell us they have the votes to do it, that in the next week or two Red China will have been granted a seat. Each year we defeat the Communist move, but by a frighteningly small margin.

Our present administration never quite comes to grips with the problem. I have a proposal to make to meet this annual challenge: the government of the United States should declare that if the United Nations votes to admit

Red China, our government will, from that moment until the action is revoked, suspend its political and financial support of the United Nations. Let us never forget that we support the United Nations not *because* it is the United Nations. The United Nations was created *to serve great human ends.* Those ends are liberty and peace. We do not want peace if, to have it, we must forego our liberty. And our liberty is imperiled if we cannot have peace. If free China's base in the Far East were undermined at the United Nations, the world organization would become an instrument for contracting liberty. If the anti-Communist alliance were to be weakened, thus encouraging the Communists in their aggressiveness, the UN would be endangering world peace. It was hardly conceived in order to support the enemies of peace and freedom.

It follows that in the interest of the very goals the United Nations was designed to serve, the United States must use every pressure at its disposal to redirect the United Nations back to the great aims stated in its Charter. Professor Hans Morgenthau of Chicago is fond of reminding us that the procedures of the United Nations are no substitute for our own policy, that our State Department cannot afford to play second fiddle to our UN delegation. *Our policy is to preserve our freedom.* The United Nations helps or hinders that policy according to the decisions it makes. If it makes decisions that militate against its own original purpose, it is no longer useful.

But what—asks the liberal lament—if every nation decided to boycott the United Nations every time the General Assembly took a move of which it disapproved? Wouldn't that mean the end of the United Nations? The answer is this, and let us not avoid stating it simply: The United States is not just "every nation." Providence has imposed upon us the task of leading the free world's fight to stay free. Ours are the principal decisions to make, and we must make them with reference to the enduring interests of freedom, even if they are not so recognized by all members of the free world itself. There would be no free country tomorrow in the world if the United States were to lose its independence of action.

Only by exercising that independence of action, even in so drastic a way as I now propose, do we continue to discharge our duty as leader and most powerful member of the free community of nations. By refusing to use the resources at our disposal, we reject our responsibilities, forfeit our strength, and weaken our cause.

The Soviet Union often talks about boycotting the United Nations. In fact it has not done so. But at that moment when withdrawal could be shown to advance the fortunes of the Soviet Revolution, the Russians would walk out. It is every nation's sovereign right to withdraw from an international body. But the point is to exercise that right, not as the Soviet Union might, as the weapon of an aggressor, but as a nation must if its vital interests are at stake.

The United States should never use its power cynically, or triflingly. We must never use the United Nations for any petty nationalistic enterprise. We do not seek to transform the United Nations into the servant of our frivolous national interest. We are willing to abide by majority votes on matters that do not involve the national security. But when the United Nations by a majority vote seriously weakens the international structure of our resistance against communism, as would be the case if the Republic of China's legitimate claim to the mainland of China were undermined, we could not afford to acquiesce simply out of a regard for the United Nations' by-laws. This is the moment where national policy must transcend international parliamentary procedure.

Fortunately, it is inconceivable that the United Nations would admit Red China if the United States took an unrelenting policy of opposition. Such a policy was taken by the Eisenhower administration—and year after year Red China lost her bid to batter her way in. Last year the Kennedy administration opposed Red China again—but not quite so forcefully—and the *status quo* was maintained by a few votes.

Does the situation change from year to year?

Has Red China become more civilized? The evidence to the contrary is striking—reports from the mainland are of the worst misery from starvation and repression in the entire history of China.

Has Red China become so strong now that we cannot afford to exclude her? The columnist Joseph Alsop, a close student of Far Eastern developments, reports, and in this others concur, that the government of Red China is weaker now than at any time in its thirteen-year history, precisely because of the costly and tragic blunders of the ruthless ideologists who have so wrecked the nation's economy and morale.

Is opposition to Red China weaker in the Far East now than last year? On the contrary, it is stronger. The swarm of refugees from Red China have carried the word of misery under Communist totalitarianism to every corner of Asia. By contrast, Formosa's economy is thriving, land redistribution has brought a wide ownership of property, and the morale of its armed forces is at an all-time high.

Why, then, should we worry year after year about the outcome of the Red China debate? In part it is because of the admission over the past two years of a dozen or so African nations whose foreign policy is oriented toward Moscow's, owing to a residual bitterness against the colonialist policies of the West. But if we are deeply convinced of the soundness of our Far Eastern position, are we prepared to allow a dozen African states (still ignorant—let's face it—of the ways of the world) to change the course of our foreign policy?

If we were truly resolved to have our way on China, we could win the votes of the African states. We could approach them in terms they understand. We could show them that the greatest colonialism ever developed, anywhere, is that of communism in China.

The important change of the recent past has been the weakness of the present administration in the field of foreign affairs—whether in Cuba, in Laos, in Outer Mongolia, or in the UN. Instead of showing resolution, what has our government done? Our Ambassador to the United Nations, Mr. Adlai Stevenson, said in January of 1961 that it was perhaps "inevitable" that Red China should be recognized. Chester Bowles, as Under-Secretary of State, was widely known to favor the admission of Red China. Many of the men who surround the President have long been associated with policies of appeasement toward Red China.

Last June the White House floated a trial balloon in

The New York Times, suggesting that we were prepared to offer a seat to Red China because we were confident she would refuse it, unless we simultaneously ejected the government of Nationalist China, and this clearly we were not prepared to do. The effect of that maneuver was to go a long way in collapsing the entire edifice of arguments, strategic and moral, which over the years the United States has painstakingly constructed against admitting Red China under any circumstance.

In July a second trial balloon was floated to the effect that by recognizing Outer Mongolia our government hoped to appease the forces clamoring for recognition of Red China.

Such a policy of appeasement and militant indecisiveness has thrown despair into the ranks of our closest allies. Our friends no longer know just exactly what are the intentions of the United States. It is on such confusion and indecision that communism thrives.

But the situation is not irreparable, and there was evidence late last year, when Red China was again rebuffed, that the back of the United States is stiffening. The answer to the forces of appeasement in the United Nations or anywhere else is a simple one. It can be expressed in just two words of one syllable each. *Say No.* We cannot cooperate in a venture in self-destruction. The United States has the power to prevent the United Nations from becoming an instrument of Communist foreign policy. We are the principal guardians of the ideals which the United Nations was formed to serve. A loyalty to those ideals requires that we refuse to cooperate in the betraying of those ideals. Such a betrayal would bring about the death of the United Nations anyway.

The true friends of international peace and freedom everywhere, including millions upon millions of Asiatics, will look upon us with gratitude and confidence if we will continue to say No to tyranny, not just this year but forever.

TEN

WHY NOT VICTORY?

STRANGELY ENOUGH, I find myself in the position of one who, over the past year, has been challenged to make a *case for victory* in a conflict with an enemy of enormous power whose undisguised aim is to conquer the United States and enslave the world. I have been challenged to explain what victory in the Communist War means, how we could achieve it, and what we would do with it after we won it. This challenge, astounding as it is, comes from the Chairman of the Senate Foreign Relations Committee—Senator J. William Fulbright of Arkansas—who reflects in his statements a policy line now being promoted within the top ranks of the Kennedy administration. Senator Fulbright, and I am sorry to say some others in positions of influence today, believes that victory in the

149

Communist War is impossible, that we must co-exist with an alien ideological power which is using every device at its command to overwhelm us, and that one of the means toward co-existence is "aggressive compromise."

I doubt if any United States Senator or government official—ever before in the history of our Republic—has been called upon to make a *case for victory* in a conflict where everything that the United States stands for today— or ever stood for in the past—is at stake. I doubt if this nation ever before has found itself in a battle for her very existence where any public official or group of public officials automatically foreclosed the possibility of victory and questioned what we would do with it if it ever were achieved.

When I realize that Senator Fulbright speaks for a sizable bloc of influence in our State Department, I begin to wonder what forces are at work among us in this hour of crisis. I wonder whether the entire scope of this protracted conflict and the dire consequences which it holds for our nation and the world's freedom have been correctly understood. I wonder whether the American people actually realize that the failure to proclaim victory as our aim in the Communist War is not just an oversight but a calculated policy of influential men. Let me state this in Senator Fulbright's own words. "Apparently we have not yet fully accepted the fact that . . . *we can hope to do little more than mitigate our problems as best we can and learn to live with them.*" Since that time, Senator Fulbright has made it plain that his method of "mitigation" would be through negotiation and compromise. This is what he proposes in the Berlin crisis, which might well serve as a terminal point in our diplomatic negotiations with Russia. The Senator apparently believes that negotiation and compromise are what we must do to "live with" communism. He assumes that the American people and the rest of the free world want to live with communism rather than risk a test of strength. He also tells us, in effect, that the price of this living is compromise—which is another way of saying that we will yield further and further to Khrushchev's demands.

But I'm getting a little ahead of myself. I believe it is important for the reader to understand how the exchange between Senator Fulbright and myself evolved. It began on June 29 of last year when the Foreign Relations Committee Chairman delivered a speech to the Senate entitled, "Some Reflections Upon Recent Events and Continuing Problems." These remarks were hailed in a certain segment of the press as a major foreign-policy declaration. Now since these "reflections" contained so many arguments for doing nothing in the Communist War but waste more and more money in the name of social reform for other nations, I felt impelled to reply. I did this in a Senate speech on July 14. I challenged the Foreign Relations Chairman to explain why his approach to the Communist War, which boils down to more and more foreign aid, has not yielded results after the expenditure of nearly a hundred billion dollars. I challenged his assertion that a successful American action in Cuba would result in alienating Latin America, Asia, and Africa. I challenged his assertion that communism ninety miles off our southern coast was not "intolerable" to the American people. I challenged his declaration that the erection of missile bases by the Communists in Cuba would not increase the danger to our national existence. And I also said that this nation needs an official declaration stating that our aim in the Communist War is victory.

Now in his response to this, Senator Fulbright ignored my question concerning the wisdom of pursuing a costly and ineffective foreign policy. He ignored quite a few other things in commenting briefly on the Senate Floor on July 24 on what he referred to as "certain themes" contained in my remarks. He was excessively bemused with one of my phrases—"total victory." He seemed to think there was something funny about it. He referred to total victory as a "stirring term with a romantic ring." He ridiculed it as something that "quickens the blood like a clarion call to arms." I suggest that ridicule is a curious attitude for an American to take when discussing victory in a struggle that means survival. It is even more curious when that American holds the influential office of Chairman of the Senate Foreign Relations Committee—and I say this whether he is referring to "total victory" or just plain "victory." There are many details of our conduct in the Communist War which invite scoffing and ridicule, but the subject of our *winning* in this desperate struggle is definitely not one of them.

The Senator from Arkansas says he does not know what victory would mean—as he puts it—"in this age of ideological conflict and nuclear weapons." Perhaps we are meant to believe that victory for the forces of freedom in the world takes on a different meaning because ideology is a factor and weapons are more powerful. If Senator Fulbright finds difficulty in understanding what victory would mean perhaps he should spend a little thought on the question of what defeat—*the only alternative to victory*—would mean. This is a frightening thought—*what would defeat mean?* But, it is one which must be considered—and considered seriously—if our national policy is anything but victory.

This is a conflict where one side or the other must win, and no amount of wishful thinking can make it otherwise. On this question, the decision is out of our hands. The rules for the conflict have been laid down by the Soviet Union through a massive design aimed at destruction of the United States and domination of the world. Against the Communist strategy as it is being pushed today, there can be no middle alternative between *a policy aimed at victory or one that would permit defeat.* There is no cozy twilight zone such as Senator Fulbright envisions where the *status quo* is maintained. We know this from what has happened to the world since the end of World War II. We have continued to delude ourselves with something called "peaceful co-existence" while communism has kept right on gobbling up one country after another. Hundreds of millions of the world's people have fallen under the yoke of communism while we have followed a useless policy of spend and drift. Now we are told that this is the only feasible approach; that we can't hope for victory; that we can't risk a war; that we couldn't cope with victory if we won it. I say this is the most dangerous kind of sheer nonsense.

If there is doubt as to what victory in the Communist War means, let me say that it means the opposite of defeat; it means freedom instead of slavery; it means the right of every man to worship God; of nations to determine their own destiny free of force and coercion. Victory in the Communist War means the sum total of all the hopes of free men throughout the world. It means human dignity, freedom of choice, the right to work. And it means peace with honor for men who prize liberty and do not fear death.

Can victory be achieved without a nuclear war? My vociferous critics would like us to believe that there can be no Communist War victory without the destruction of civilization. This is precisely what the Communists would like us to believe. Their whole line of attack, through propaganda and adroit economic, political, and military moves, is directed toward making us think in terms of fear. They want to make sure that we believe the risk is too great to employ our strength. Their purpose is intimidation and it is working too well.

Indeed, a decisive victory over the Communists is possible. It won't be easy because we have lost too much valuable time and too many golden opportunities. But it can be done with the proper integrated strategy—a strategy that *aims at victory*; that retains our economic strength; that incorporates the principles of political, military, economic, and psychological strength in meeting Communist challenges and in presenting some challenges of our own. Those who argue against any use of strength, against any military risk, against any unilateral action fail to understand that political victory in the Communist War is the only way to avoid a strictly military solution of the East-West crisis. It involves some risk, but experience shows us that this risk is greatly overexaggerated. Every time we have stood up to the Communists they have backed down. Our trouble is we have not stood up to them enough.

Despite the arguments of Communists and left-wing propagandists who want us to believe that the present ideological struggle will inevitably lead to a shooting war, just the reverse is true. A shooting war can only be avoided by *winning the Communist War.* And unless we win this struggle, we will be an easy push-over for the Khrushchevs, the Castros, and the Mao Tse-tungs when they decide the time is ripe to shift their strategy into a shooting phase. Senator Fulbright has joined the ranks of those who would paralyze the foreign policy of this nation by advancing the alternatives that either you accommodate the Soviet Union—or you fight a nuclear war. These are the alternatives which are stressed every time the Communists seek to advance their position. The essential weakness of this reasoning lies in accepting the enemy's terms—that the only alternative to self-destruction is to yield. First, we yield on one issue—unimportant, it appears, in context of such a horrible alternative as nuclear war. Then on a second and a third and a fourth, ad infinitum. So what is finally left to us except the same terrible dilemma we were confronted with on that first day when the enemy said: Yield or die?

If we could finally satisfy the enemy's appetite by giving him one city or one country or one territory, who among us, Democrat or Republican, liberal or conservative, would not be tempted to say: Let them, in the name of peace and freedom for the rest of the world, let them, once and for all, have their way and be done with it. But this is not possible. We are dealing with an enemy whose appetite is insatiable, whose creed demands slavery for everyone, Americans included. The more we give in to that enemy, the more he wants; and the more we give in to him, the more he is encouraged to demand.

My opponents adroitly try to make it appear that I am

in favor of nuclear war, that I would make war the prime instrument of our policy. I can't imagine what makes them think that. No one values life more than do I. Would I take satisfaction from exchanging my pleasant life, my family, my freedom, for a nuclear graveyard? Certainly not. But that does not mean that I am prepared to assure the enemy that, under *no* circumstances, will we *ever* consider war. If we are not prepared, under any circumstances, ever to fight a nuclear war, we might just as well do as the pacifists and the collaborationists propose—dump our entire arsenal into the ocean.

But my critics have proposed no such venture in national suicide. They want us to save our bombs. Only they apparently want us to act as though we did not have them— because the mere thought of having them terrifies those who are dedicated to the principle of co-existence. Thus, we are supposed to eliminate our possession of nuclear weapons from our consciousness in discussing the formulation of American foreign policy.

If victory is not our official aim, then there would appear to be no point in bringing all our arguments—be they military, economic, political, or psychological—to bear on the side of freedom. But can we be sure that if we completely eliminate the possible use of nuclear weapons the Communists will follow suit? Can we risk our future and the future of mankind on exclusive emphasis on conventional rather than ultimate weapons? Can we make any assumptions that would diminish our strength—in any field —when dealing with the Communists? Merely to ask the questions is to answer them. We can assume *nothing* where the Communist leaders are concerned. We can trust *noth-*

ing that the Communist leaders say. We can accept *nothing* that the Communist leaders sign as a conclusive guarantee.

The Communist plan of world conquest makes the element of time a vital factor. Time is running out on the West while it is working in favor of international communism—at least under our present policy. I would remind you the policy we are following today is the same one which we have followed—with a few exceptions—since the end of World War II. It is the policy of spending in the hope of gaining allies. It is the policy which has permitted the Communists to gain in almost every area of the world while the cause of freedom has been losing.

I want to emphasize this time factor particularly in the light of what Senator Fulbright sees as our objective. He says that "total victory" is a process. And he defines that process as one *"of civilizing international relations and of bringing them gradually under a world-wide regime of law and order and peaceful procedures for the redress of legitimate grievances."*

If this is our objective, what is our hope of achieving it? This just says that the United States should work for the establishment of some kind of international super-state whose members would behave in a civilized and peaceful way toward each other. At the very least this would take several centuries. And we have no assurance that the time will *ever* come when all other states will want to behave peacefully toward each other. The lessons of history are all against it. There have always been men and states that would not hesitate to use arms to advance their national policies and defend their special interests.

A world without arms, a world living peacefully and adjusting its grievances in a global regime of law and order is more than an objective. It is a glorious dream, a kind of utopia. Even if it were practical, such an objective has no direct application to the urgent problems which beset the world today. We haven't the time for implementing dreams right now. We must deal with reality, the ever-present threat of Communist tyranny which is *not* going to submit to the kind of civilizing Senator Fulbright envisions.

Suppose there is a big fire in your neighborhood. What do you think about first? You think of saving your house from destruction and your family from death. And if the flames have already enveloped your garden fence, do you lose time planning to build a dream house next year or next decade in a nonexistent fire-proof city in a theoretical country? Of course, you don't. You go to work fighting the flames to save the house you've already got in the city and country—no matter what their imperfections—where you live now.

This is the way it is today with our country and with the world. There is a fire, and its Communist flames are threatening to destroy the American way of life. Not next year, or in the next decade, or in a future century, but right now—today. These ugly Red flames are already brushing our shores and they continue to rage unchecked.

This is no time for an American foreign-policy objective designed to erect an impractical international dream city of the future. Our objective must be the practical means of dousing the fire and smothering the flames of international communism.

So what can we do? Our job, first and foremost, is to persuade the enemy that we would rather follow the world to Kingdom Come than consign it to Hell under communism. Having made that clear, we must seize opportunities as they arise to protect freedom and demonstrate our strengths. Many such opportunities have arisen in the past, a few of which we have used to good advantage. For example, we were told by the weak of heart and the peddlers of despair that unless we yielded Quemoy and Matsu, the islands off the Chinese coast, to the Communists, a terrible war would result. The Eisenhower administration said, in effect, very well, if the Communist world chooses to go to war to occupy these islands, then that's the way it will have to be. But the Communist world did not so choose, and Quemoy and Matsu are free today. And they will be free tomorrow and just as long as our resolution lasts.

This sequence of events was repeated in Lebanon. We sent in Marines there against the trembling advice of those who fear any display of determination and strength. And Lebanon is free today. We acted from strength, too, when threatened Berlin was saved by our airlift in 1948, and at least half of Berlin remains free today. In Korea, we responded in June of 1950 with courage and a commitment but we allowed the fear-mongers among us to whittle that initial commitment to victory down to an acceptance of a humiliating stalemate.

On the other hand, our resolve was not strong enough in Cuba to back our intent with the strength required. The result is that Cuba languishes in chains while a Communist dictator thumbs his nose at the United States and plays the enemy's game to the hilt. And when my critics

worry lest we alienate the rest of Latin America by taking
affirmative action in Cuba, I am sure Castro guffaws. Much
of Latin America has already been alienated by the timidity
and ineffectiveness of our American policy. The Latins cannot understand why a world power, such as the United
States, allows a two-bit Kremlin stooge to spit in our eye.
And they wonder what source of support we could possibly
be to them when communism pushes its expansion program throughout the Western Hemisphere. They see us
weak and baffled in an area of vital concern, not only to
them but to our own existence.

Must we surrender Laos, too? Is that the fixed convic-
tion of Senator Fulbright when he worries lest we commit
American soldiers to a jungle war? Are there not Free
Chinese, South Vietnamese, South Koreans, Filipinos,
and Japanese who would fight if the United States gave
them backing? Have we ever asked them?

When Senator Fulbright questions what we would do
with victory if we won it, he implies that any doubt or difficulty on this score becomes, per se, an argument against
winning. He asks whether we would occupy Russia and
China and launch a program to re-educate the Russians
and the Chinese in the ways of democracy. The answer to
this is simply "no." We would not have to occupy China
and Russia because the vast majority of the people in both
of these countries are not Communists. They will, with
proper guidance, take care of their own freedom once they
are released from the iron grip of Communist dictatorship.
But even if this weren't true, the mere fact that victory
would pose problems is not reason to submit to slavery.

In this same connection, Senator Fulbright says that our

victories in World War I and World War II "offer little encouragement." I assume that his reference is to the fact that, having won the wars, we lost the peace—at Versailles, at Yalta, Teheran, and Potsdam. I won't argue with him there. We did lose the peace in both instances. But if our victories in the two world wars "offer little encouragement," what would defeat at the hands of the Kaiser or at the hands of Adolf Hitler have offered? Because we lost the peace after World War I and World War II, should we not try to win the struggle in which we are presently engaged?

Against the advice of those who counsel inaction because of the risk, let me ask, when has Western resolution backed up by Western disposition to use its total resources ever been defied by the Communist empire? The answer is never—not once. The rulers of the Kremlin would sooner reduce their territory to the ancient state of Muscovy than to die fighting for their ideology. Their doctrine does not call for fatal acts of heroism. Their credo is: "Live to fight (subvert) another day."

In the final analysis the choice is not yield or fight a nuclear war. It is: *win, or fight a nuclear war*. For a nuclear war we shall certainly have to fight, from whatever beleaguered outpost we are reduced to occupying, if we continue to yield, piece by piece, all over the world. Finally, in desperation, we would see the horrible alternatives clearly in view—a violent act of nuclear aggression or surrender. Our only hope is to proclaim victory as our aim and then to press boldly and unremittingly on all fronts— always *prepared* to fight and making sure the Communists always know we are prepared to fight.

And, in laying that groundwork, there are a number of immediate steps we should take to re-orient our policy for maximum United States effectiveness in the Communist War. They include the following:

1. We must stop believing that our primary objective must be to humor the public opinion of neutral or uncommitted nations rather than to defend our strategic interests, cooperate closely with our allies, and advance our positions of strength. This we must do the more readily because much of this so-called opinion which entrances our co-existence proponents is fabricated by the Communists to our detriment. We must realize that we have no proper method by which we can judge what public opinion really is throughout the world.

2. We must stop lying to ourselves and our friends about disarmament. We must stop advancing the cause of the Soviet Union by playing along with this great Communist-inspired deception. We must abandon the illusion that the Soviets, in their disarmament policies, are interested in furthering peace rather than baiting a trap for us. Their objective is to contrive *our* unilateral disarmament while they continue to arm themselves secretly as fast as they can.

It is not "dialectics" but schizophrenia when we increase our military budget by 15 percent and the Soviets theirs by 33 percent while, at the same time, we proclaim that disarmament is our highest goal and a practical method of solving the present conflict. The American people can stand the truth, but they cannot prosper under an official policy of self-deception.

3. We must not again abandon nuclear testing. This is the worst and most transparent trap into which the United

States has fallen during the course of the Cold War. A ban does nothing but serve the Soviet Union to improve its nuclear weapons by clandestine testing, to stop our own advances in offensive and defensive nuclear technology and, ultimately, lead to a situation where we wake up confronted with superior Soviet weapons.

4. We must stop negotiating about things that are nonnegotiable, such as the rights of our allies, compromises of our security, treaties like the test ban which can be neither controlled nor enforced. We must not deceive ourselves and our friends into believing that nuclear weapons and modern technology can be negotiated out of existence.

5. We must stop helping communism, whether by trade, political concessions, technical disclosures, soft talk in the United Nations, recognition of Outer Mongolia, pilgrimages to Moscow, or support for revolutionaries of the Castro type.

6. We must avoid economic collapse by scaling down extravagant and useless domestic programs, and halt the squandering of our money on unrealistic world-wide aid programs.

In this mortal struggle there is no substitute for victory. The way of strength is not an easy way. It is a hard course requiring determination and difficult decisions involving considerable risk. But it is the way of peace, not war, of freedom, not slavery. It must be the way of all Americans, Republicans and Democrats alike, the way of all free people with the will to remain free.

ELEVEN

A NEW KIND OF WAR

WE ARE THE WORLD'S most powerful nation, both economically and in the military sense—yet we feel exposed and insecure and unsure. With the other leading free nations we have formed alliances which are capable of almost any endeavor, but we find ourselves losing one position after another throughout the world.

Why are we losing? Why are we paralyzed in a posture of global ineffectiveness?

The answer is that we have prepared our defense and offense for one kind of war while the enemy is fighting a wholly different kind of war—a war for which we have as yet devised no over-all design or strategy.

Our wars in the past have all sprung from clashes of interests between nations. They have involved international power rivalries and have concerned all the ingredients of such power, things like boundaries, territories, spheres of influence, armaments, and prestige. In these conflicts, military war became the ultimate determinant of power. A shooting war, in this context, was meant to lead ultimately to peace, that is, to the re-establishment of normal relations with the enemy country. Consequently, these wars were never total, in the sense that they aimed at relative power and not at the enemy's actual existence.

We are conducting the Communist War today as though it were a clash with the power drive of an ambitious nation, namely Russia. And, in this, we have done all the conventional things. We have strengthened our military system, evolved alliances with our friends, sought to contain the enemy, and even striven to out-maneuver him at the conference table. We have done everything but understand how to use our power in a new kind of war.

If the Communist War were a conventional struggle, the measures we have taken ought to be sufficient to yield some dividends on the side of freedom. But because this is not a conventional struggle, and because we have not devised a total strategy aimed at victory, we are falling ever further behind.

We are losing the struggle today because we are mistaking both the enemy and the Communist War for something they are not. The conflict in which we are engaged is not limited to a dispute between great nations over boundaries and territories, because the enemy is not in any real sense the government of a nation. Where we are inclined to think in terms of territorial losses, the Communists think in terms of destroying the institutions and tenets of freedom. True enough, the Communists rule Russia. But this is a power structure that transcends national boundaries and looks primarily to other interests than those of the territory under its government. The leaders of the Communist Party not only rule Russia but they are, in actual fact, the directors of a militant world-wide enterprise aimed at destroying existing social orders throughout the world in order to make room for the establishment of Communist rule. In this context, their allies become chaos and confusion, no matter who generates it, whether it be UN troops in Katanga, or Indian troops in Goa. For the Communists, Russia has become a power base and an effective instrument for their designs, and this is the reason why the interests of the Communist Party always become identified with those of Russia.

The Communists view their war as something more than just the temporary destruction of a rival nation's power. Theirs is a war aimed at the social, economic, political, and military fiber of all non-Communist societies as such. And they do not regard this war as an abnormal break in peaceful relations, a temporary pursuit aimed at a temporary objective. They believe that all human society is split into warring elements, that this warfare will continue indefinitely, and that it can be used by them to further the destruction of freedom wherever it exists. To them "peace" has only one value—as a useful stratagem for lulling anti-Communist societies until such time as the Communists wish to return to other devices such as terror, intimidation, aggression, and infiltration.

Now in the struggle which we call the Cold War, the Communists use the power and resources of Russia, but not merely for the sake of Russia's national interests nor for the traditional objectives of international power conflicts. The aim of their drive is not the boundary that separates them from other nations, but rather the cement that holds these other societies together. When Russia shook the world with its sudden resumption of nuclear tests and its explosion of high-megaton bombs last year, their purpose was to shake that cement, those foundations, of the free societies.

I do not contend that territorial control is of no interest to the Communists in their conduct of the Communist War. My point is that territorial control to them is merely one of a number of power positions, of which at times others might interest them to a more pronounced degree. Military force also is a means to an end with the Communists, but it never is considered alone as decisive. It invariably is employed in combination with political techniques for subjecting people's wills. And this is particularly confusing to us because in the conventional manner of our thinking we are inclined to regard international war as a decisive move after which we would expect to enter into normal, if strained, relations with our opponents. The Communists see things from an entirely different point of view. They hold that the conflict can end only when our public order is totally destroyed, our institutions thoroughly subverted, our loyalties completely dissolved, our values fully denied, and our communal identity forever wiped out. They do not conceive of a reconciliating peace with us either as the aftermath of war or through some other kind of fundamental adjustment of viewpoints and objectives. They are conducting a total war of total negation for which the experience of international relations has not prepared us. They aim at people, individual people, whom they seek to deprive of all protective layers of institutions, loyalties, and companionship, in order to deliver them naked and isolated into the hands of the Party's dictatorial rule.

We must realize once and for all that our enemy is not a nation but a political movement made up of ideologically possessed people who have organized themselves as an armed force and secured control over entire countries. They have cadres in every country and use Moscow as their command post. We miss the point if we see our opponents merely as aggressor nations. A Communist occupying a position of power in the Congo is just as much our enemy as the power clique ruling Soviet Russia or Communist China.

And we subvert our own cause when we exert military and monetary pressure on pro-Western leaders to make them submit to coalition arrangements with Communists. We have made this mistake in Katanga by supporting military action to force Tshombe to join a government which includes the Communist Gizenga. We are also making this mistake in Laos, where pressure is being brought on the anti-Communist Prince Boun Oum to force him into a coalition with a Communist leader and a pro-Communist "neutral." This amounts to "making book" with the enemy, for such coalitions are at the very best merely way stations on the road to Communist domination. Every time we insist on a coalition government with a Communist and a neutral we automatically set up a two-to-one situation against freedom.

Our objective must be the destruction of the enemy as

an ideological force possessing the means of power. Our purpose must be the world-wide defense of human society against a nihilistic force. Where the Communists seek to destroy the live tissue of social order, we must seek to destroy the decomposing virus. And our effort calls for a basic commitment in the name of victory which says we will never reconcile ourselves to the Communists' possession of power of any kind in any part of the world.

Strategically, our program must be directed toward the removal of Communists from power, whether they hold it ninety miles off our southern coast or in distant Laos and Vietnam. It must be a combined operation utilizing variegated and flexible methods which are adjustable to the possibilities of different times and places. We must mount an intellectual counterattack against the enemy's ideology, and this must combine legal and organizational methods designed both to hold disputed areas of society and advance into enemy-held positions. We must act boldly when military action is indicated and direct it, not against nations, but against Communists in power. Our armaments, thus, should include the tools for this kind of pin-pointed action as well as the nuclear power to deter the Communists from making an attempt to use the Russian or Chinese nations for the advancement of the Party's designs.

We must not think of the international Communist conspiracy as a "system" that merely sees things differently from us. If we do, we automatically give it a status and dignity which it does not deserve and which can only result in our underestimating the threat. Communism and the slavery which it seeks to impose on the world is not a "system" to be dealt with in the conventional, time-tested manner of the past. It is a disease attacking and eating away at a human society and human freedom. It must be attacked as a scourge with all the weapons that we possess. Because communism is the sum of "total negation" in human society, efforts we bring against it must have a totality of both design and execution.

It does not help any to adopt the false notion that communism is spawned by poverty, disease, and other similar social and economic conditions. Communism is spawned by Communists, and Communists alone. When we adopt the idea that the only way effectively to halt the spread of communism is to terminate social and economic conditions that do not make for universal ease and comfort, we are adopting defeat. *For we will never even make a dent in these conditions in the immediate future no matter how much foreign aid and technical help we spread around the world.* All we do when we make this consideration pivotal in our Communist War efforts is to diffuse our strength and weaken our assault on the prime target, which is Communist power. I certainly don't think for one minute that there is anything unworthy in a goal which envisions a world without poverty, disease, and filth, and where all international relations are humanized and conducted in good faith. But this is not the practical objective which we should be pursuing in the Communist War. It is a dream for the future of mankind, a dream which can never come to pass if we do not apply ourselves immediately to the first objective—the removal of Communist power.

Now when we make the disease of communism our enemy, always recognizing that the disease has corrupted many governments, we make it abundantly clear that we do not seek the changing of boundaries or spheres of influence in our favor. We seek rather the removal of Communists from positions of power wherever they are able to thwart the natural will of peoples and impose a despotic and tyrannical system which denies all the basic tenets of human freedom and decency.

This must be our basic purpose in a resolute, never-changing strategy for victory. This is what I believe is needed to give over-all direction and reason to our efforts. It is the funnel through which every move we make in the Communist War can be brought to bear on the enemy with maximum force and effect. It would remove the confusion, the working at cross-purposes which is inherent in our present policy and which has so deeply frustrated the American people.

With such a purpose and strategy, we would quickly see the fallacy in lending any kind of aid to the enemy. The enemy is just as much an enemy in the Communist government of Yugoslavia as it is in North Korea and in North Vietnam. All aid to Tito and other Communist or semi-Communist regimes must be halted in recognition of the fact that such funds and such supplies could much better be used in the cause of freedom elsewhere. We have been duped too long by wishful thinking that Communist governments which disagree with Moscow are potential allies and, as such, must be fed billions of dollars in American aid. We are at war with an evil and the evil is communism —all kinds and varieties. That evil must be opposed and fought at every turn regardless of whether it happens to be in the Kremlin's good graces. At the very least it must be denied our help, either directly in the form of economic and military aid or indirectly in the form of increased trade with the Communist bloc.

With such a purpose and strategy, we would be through with half-measures such as we used in the Cuban invasion. We would never embark on any venture against Communist power without using all the strength necessary to make it succeed. We would rid ourselves of blind devotion to the United Nations. We would stop guessing at how much of a nuclear weapons gain the Communists had achieved in recent months and begin our own atmospheric tests immediately. We would face up quickly and finally to the fact that the whole idea of disarmament is ridiculous at this time because the Communist masters cannot even think about disarming while revolt lies just beneath the surface of life in their satellite nations.

In summary then, let me emphasize the following points:

1. Whether we like it or not we are engaged in a death struggle with an enemy which is waging a new kind of total war and which has declared its intention to bury us.

2. The conventional attitudes and weapons of the past must be revised and drawn into a new strategic design if we are to meet the threat posed by a tyrannical force of global dimensions.

3. That the enemy is Communist ideology and power, and must be opposed with a total concept, whether it exists in Yugoslavia, Moscow, East Berlin, or North Vietnam.

4. That coalition government in today's world is a tactic of the enemy. When the Communists join in any kind of a coalition government, it is always with the intention of dominating and taking over that government.

5. That the last thing we should do is assist the enemy by

sending money, weapons, food, and other goods to Communist nations regardless of whether they have had a falling out with the power clique in the Kremlin.

I believe the American people have the right to know the truth, as unhappy as that truth might be, in the light of current world developments. It is insulting to our intelligence as well as dangerous for men in influential positions to run around arguing that communism has not gained since 1945 and that the West is, in fact, winning the Communist War.

The tragic fact is that during 1961 communism made its greatest gains since the fall of China. And it will make greater gains in the immediate future if we don't recognize the enemy for what it is, proclaim victory as our goal, and adapt our strength to the task of opposing Communist power wherever it exists.

TWELVE

THE SCIENTISTS
AND THE GENERALS

AMERICA MUST BEGIN to win by making up its mind to win; and I am frankly appalled, in reading the statements of our leaders, that this determination is singularly lacking in our announced objectives. What accounts for this? Why is it that we follow a no-win policy? Is it because we have confused the Communist War with a species of peace? Is it because we are afraid of Communist military power at a time when we are materially equipped as no other nation on earth to meet the threat? Is it because we feel that a policy based on strength which recognizes the proper uses of power would lead to a shooting war?

Our floundering stems, at least in part, from a fundamental doubt in the minds of many about the propriety of bringing our full military weight to bear on the objective. This was touched on earlier when we considered the U-2 incident and our attitudes and reactions to it. Now I should like to explore further the thought that this country is suffering from a kind of split personality which had its roots in our use of the atomic bomb at Hiroshima.

Think back to that time if you will. Almost overnight the American people were made aware of a new and terrifying dimension in power and destruction. A single bomb had laid waste an entire city and wiped out more than 90,000 human beings. The flash had been many times the brilliance of the sun. The detonation had sounded like God's own thunder.

To the mind of the layman it seemed, in actual fact, like taking an advance peek at eternity. To say the very least, the power and destructive qualities of the atomic bomb were awe-inspiring in a way that had a heavy immediate impact and a long-lasting effect on both the minds and the consciences of the American people.

At that time, our papers and magazines were filled with speculation as to whether man had not, finally, encroached on the preserves of the Almighty with his scientific progress. Questions were raised, not only in military and scientific forums, but in the pulpits of the nation, in classrooms, in PTA meetings, in union halls—in fact, every place where men met and exchanged views—and these questions ranged across the whole spectrum of man's experience on earth.

And, all of a sudden—again seemingly overnight—the scientist became almost a species of deity. A special reverence was conferred on the scientific community not only for what it had wrought from nuclear fission but for the mere fact that the members of this community understood the phenomenon. What was incomprehensible to the average man on the street had its origins in scientific equations and formulas propounded by a special breed of human being. Naturally, the words and opinions of the scientists became heavy with significance and portent. They were avidly sought and their words just as avidly absorbed by a nation of laymen which soon began to bestow on the scientific community credit for omnipotence in other fields, fields formerly reserved to diplomats, military leaders, and philosophers. Because the scientists had perfected what then was considered to be the ultimate weapon of war, people with a longing for absolutes began to believe that they had the answers for other problems—many of them completely unrelated to science, and some not adaptable to the scientific mind.

It was at this time that a schism appeared in the scientific community which split the men who had developed the atomic bomb into two groups. One of these groups held that the facts of nature would lend themselves to exploration by scientists throughout the world regardless of their nationality or political persuasion. They contended that the Communists ultimately would have the secret of the atom bomb. And they argued that our job was to continue to improve our nuclear technology as rapidly as we could so that we could maintain a commanding lead over the enemies of freedom.

But the other, and far more vocal, group of scientists developed a natural guilt complex. The members of this group spent much of their time publicly lamenting their role in the development of a weapon they glumly predicted would spell the end of mankind. They seemed to be strangling in a personal mantle of guilt, which appeared to assail them to a far greater degree after the fact than when they were, in actuality, working to develop the A-bomb. There was a presumptuousness and conceit inherent in this attitude which went, for the most part, unnoticed by the American public. It was as though these scientists were saying that without them the secrets of nuclear chain reaction would never have come to light, and that without them no further progress could be made. It seems never to have occurred to them that God does not confine his special gifts to a few men and that if these particular scientists hadn't unlocked the secrets of the atom other men would have.

This split in the scientific community spread over into other areas of public policy and for a time seriously threatened the continued security of the nation in what became known as the Great Debate over development of the H-bomb, or as it is presently known, the nuclear bomb. It was during this debate that the scientists with the guilt feelings made their big stand against the United States developing and building the hydrogen bomb, a weapon so much more powerful that it had to be triggered by the kind of bomb we exploded at Hiroshima.

Now just suppose for a moment that we had listened to this group. Assume that we had, in an unrealistic and dangerous excess of international morality, called off all nuclear research and development. Suppose we had stopped working after the development of the A-bomb and never developed a nuclear bomb such as we have today. Then, just consider our feelings when Soviet Russia began exploding her 25- and 50- and 100-megaton bombs. Had we listened to the "guilt group" among the scientists we would be, at this very moment, at the mercy of the Communists.

In retrospect, we have every reason to be thankful that the decision was made to go ahead with the development of the nuclear bomb. In the light of what has happened in Russian scientific development and in the aggressive thrusts of Communist power throughout the world, we know now that it would have been nothing short of national suicide to have taken the advice of the moralists and scientists with a "guilt complex."

But, even so, the Great Debate and the decision which followed it had the effect of deepening a sense of guilt in many Americans who sincerely hoped that a way could be found to bring a halt safely to the development and production of all nuclear weapons.

There is in existence today—and growing all the time— a new literature of military strategy which is not the work of military men at all but of newly minted "nuclear philosophers" whose backgrounds are scientific and whose humanitarian distaste for the bomb is manifest in everything they write.

One of the disturbing philosophical assumptions behind this new literature of strategy is that the so-called rigid military mind may, by pushing the button that sends a bomb winging on its way toward Moscow, trigger a nuclear counterattack that will destroy our own cities and, in fact, all of life here in the United States.

The unhappy results of this kind of thinking are two in number: (1) the military leader is set up as a straw-man villain, eager and at liberty to press the button and plunge the world into an atomic holocaust, and (2) nuclear weapons must never, never be used by the United States—in fact we must never even think of using them—because their use will prompt a counterattack which will destroy the United States.

These conclusions are both erroneous and dangerous. In the first place, no military man, no matter how high his rank, can "push the button" or give the order to do so. The order must come from the President of the United States. Secondly, there is an erroneous assumption behind this downgrading of military men that they are somehow elevated second-class citizens, that a general or admiral is "nothing but a fighting man," that he sees solutions to all international problems in term of dropping bombs, that he is, in short, a tiger on a leash.

The nuclear philosophers on the left who paint this distorted image must know better. The admirals and generals of today are hardly blood-thirsty pirates wearing black patches and gripping cutlasses in their teeth. They are keen, competent, well-rounded, fully educated human beings searching just as hard as our diplomats for peaceful solutions to international problems. In this day and age *when military power is the greatest deterrent to war that we have,* it is accurate to say that our generals and admirals are, in fact, strategists of peace as well as experts on war.

An extraordinary example of two military men working through strength for peace is that of General (then President) Eisenhower and Admiral Arthur Radford (then Chairman of the Joint Chiefs) preventing the Red Chinese from taking Quemoy and Matsu, the islands that the President and the Admiral decided in early 1955 were necessary for our defense of Formosa and the Pescadores. Despite the frightened bleats of the liberal-radicals who contended that the off-shore islands were as close to the China mainland as Staten Island is to New York City and therefore really should belong to Red China, and despite the heavy shelling of Quemoy and Matsu from the mainland and what seemed like ominous invasion preparations, the President and the Admiral simply said we would fight if the islands were attacked. The Chinese Communists backed down. By this show of strength, the President and the Admiral avoided war rather than risked it.

A much more disastrous effect of this doctrine of fear that is being spread by the new nuclear philosophers is this omnipresent implication *that no matter what happens we cannot use the bomb.* Needless to say, we all hope that a nuclear bomb will never be dropped in anger on this earth. We spend much of our time and energy trying to prevent such a tragedy. But to state publicly, or even mildly suggest, that we will never use the greatest deterrent force that we possess is, in effect, to invite an all-out Communist attack on our way of life, our freedom, and our country. The surest path to nuclear war is for us to lull Russia into the misconception that we will never use the nuclear weapons. If and when so convinced, Russia will attack; and then, in defense of our freedom and our way of life, we will definitely strike back with all the power at our command. The bombs will fall.

These attacks on the men in uniform—particularly those in positions of responsibility and command—began early in the life of the new administration. They began with the censoring of some remarks prepared for delivery by Adm. Arleigh A. Burke, then Chief of Naval Operations. And this has set the pattern for repeated interference by civilian officials of the new administration in the realm of public utterances by our military leaders.

Another move came in the Congress of the United States when a member of the Senate Foreign Relations Committee attempted by innuendo to saddle the Joint Chiefs of Staff with blame for the Cuban invasion fiasco. This was an especially devious attack since the member in question emerged from an executive session of the Committee and demanded the resignation of the Chairman of the Joint Chiefs. He left the erroneous impression that something had been revealed at the closed session which would warrant such a demand. Of course, the demand was not honored. It wasn't even taken seriously. But it had the effect of undermining public confidence in the Joint Chiefs of Staff and our military leadership at a particularly critical time in our history. It served no purpose but further to confuse the entire Cuban situation, which has never been clarified to the satisfaction of the American people. And I would remind you that only the national administration can do this job—the job of assigning the responsibility for a chaotic, poorly planned, and totally inadequate venture.

Along this same line, it is now becoming popular in the national government to investigate and censor military men who have any words of warning to say in public about Communist influences in American life. I cannot help but wonder what kind of struggle we are waging when it becomes a censorable offense to discuss the tactics of the enemy. Regardless of what the official policy might be, there can be no denying that communism is our enemy.

Even though our peril is great, we find a situation developing where military commanders are in danger of being charged with "right-wing political theories" if they have the temerity to call attention to our danger and point out the methods used most successfully by our enemies.

Curiously enough, we find the Defense Department today threatening to crack down on Cold War seminars held by military commanders to increase public awareness "of the danger of the Communist menace."

Perhaps the most ridiculous, farfetched attack of this kind was made on Gen. Curtis LeMay, Air Force Chief of Staff. It was based on a published report that the General had told a Senator's wife that a nuclear war was inevitable within a certain period of time. Now as ridiculous as the source of this report was, General LeMay actually had to defend himself against the charge and make it plain that he had never made any such statement.

Only recently, Lt. Gen. Arthur G. Trudeau, Army Chief of Research and Development, testified at a Senate subcommittee hearing that his speeches were being censored by "majors and civilians" and doubted the wisdom of this kind of arbitrary limitation of his freedom of speech. At the same time General Eisenhower suggested strongly that leading military men assume a major role in warning the public of the dangers from international communism. He questioned "the desirability of requiring topmost governmental officials, whether military or civilian, to submit their proposed public statements for what amounts to censorship of content—as distinguished from security matters." Finally, he deplored any effort "to thrust the military behind an 'American iron curtain.' "

Every category of thinking American has its place and its important function. The scientists are terribly important to the welfare of America and the world. So are our military men. If the situation just described were reversed —if the military men were encroaching on diplomatic territory, mouthing dangerous philosophies, and trying to muzzle the scientists—then I would holler just as vehemently that the generals and admirals had better simmer down and tend to their knitting.

There are two important and related points involved here—(1) the balanced view and (2) freedom of speech. Both are absolutely essential to our continued existence as a free nation.

THIRTEEN

A FINAL WORD

READING OVER what I have written it strikes me that my tone may be lacking in humility. I don't know all the answers and I have very little patience with those who pretend they do.

None of us here in Washington knows all or even half of the answers. You people out there in the fifty states had better understand that. If you love your country, don't depend on handouts from Washington for your information. If you cherish your freedom, don't leave it all up to BIG GOVERNMENT.

Your representatives in the nation's capital are not unlike you—with your doubts and faults and frailties. What was it my prep school football coach used to say in the locker room before the game to quiet our fears about

the monsters we were about to meet on the gridiron?
"Those guys are human, they put on their pants one leg
at a time just like you do."

Your Congressman, your Senators, your Cabinet members, and your President are human. I dare say—though I
could not prove it to be a fact—that they all put their
trousers on one leg at a time.

Being human, they need help. Your help. After all,
you elect them. They are responsible to you. But the
reverse is also true. You must be responsible to them.

How?

Stop thinking that Russia and peace and nuclear bombs
and balancing the budget are *their* problems down in
Washington. These are your problems and only you can
solve them.

If you don't know anything about the budget or taxes
(except how to pay them) or where your money goes, you
had better find out.

If you don't know anything about the Communist conspiracy, if you think Karl Marx is Groucho's brother, if
what Khrushchev is doing to the world escapes your attention because you turn right to the sports page (I turn
right to the sports page but then I reluctantly thumb to
the front of the paper), then you are not being responsible
to the people you elect.

Representing people in Washington is a tricky business.
We, the elected, half lead and we half follow. We follow
you who elect us, trying as best we can to represent your
ideas and desires. But at the same time we lead you, or
we are supposed to, toward wise decisions and sound
policies. The conservatives, however, don't lead you way

out into left field as do some of our radical-liberal brethren. Conservatives have a great faith in the sound common sense of the American people and a legitimate concern about getting too far ahead of popular sentiment. There is a patronizing expression I hear too often around Washington: "The people aren't ready for it." Something "the people aren't ready for" usually turns out to be a wild liberal panacea.

An expression I hear very often *away* from Washington is "What can I do? After all, I'm just one little vote." "Fiddlesticks!" as all our grandmothers used to say. You are 180,000,000 voices and I'm just one little Senator. Another indication of this "little me, who am I?" attitude is a question I sometimes hear that goes like this: "Senators (or Congressmen or the President) never really look at their mail, do they? That's why I never write."

Senators not only read their mail but they count it lovingly, think about it, are guided by it, worry over it, and answer it. By our mail we know what you are thinking back home, what you want of us, and what your reaction was to our last speech or vote in Congress. And, incidentally, from our mail we may get an inkling as to what our chances are of getting re-elected.

Every step forward that this country takes is either started by the people or endorsed by the people. A democracy is only as sound as its electorate is active and well informed.

For too many years in this country, the conservatives have hidden under stones as if they really believed they were the fossils the radicals said they were. A conservative in Washington felt sometimes that he had no constituency, that he was talking to himself or just to fill pages in the *Congressional Record.*

Well—the fossils have climbed out from under the stones and brushed themselves off. They find to their astonishment that the radicals are really the ones in an advanced state of calcification and the conservatives—wonder of wonders—wear the new look.

Something new that is also old is on the move in this land of ours. The rich traditions of the American past are reasserting themselves. It had to happen sooner or later.

BIBLIOGRAPHY AND SUGGESTED READING

William McGovern, *Strategic Intelligence and the Shape of Tomorrow*, Henry Regnery Company, Chicago, 1961

William Henry Chamberlain, *The Evolution of a Conservative*, Henry Regnery Company, Chicago, 1959

"Two Worlds in Conflict," a publication vol. BB, Course 3; Extension Course Institute, USAF Air University, Maxwell Air Force Base, Montgomery, Alabama

Eugene M. Emme, Major, USAFR, *The Impact of Air Power*, D. Van Nostrand Company, Inc., Princeton, 1959

Robert Strausz-Hupe, William R. Kintner, Stefan T. Possony, *Protracted Conflict* and *A Forward Strategy for America*, Harper & Brothers, New York

Salvador de Madariaga, *The Blowing Up of the Parthenon, or How to Lose the Cold War*, Frederick A. Praeger, New York, 1961

David J. Dallin, *Soviet Foreign Policy After Stalin*, J. B. Lippincott Company, Philadelphia, 1961

Tsolak Stepanyan, "Socialism and Communism," USSR Illustrated Monthly, Washington, D.C.

John Acton, EED, *Lectures on Modern History*, St. Martin's Press, New York, 1956

Arnold J. Toynbee, *A Study of History*, Vol. XII, Reconsiderations, Oxford University Press, New York, 1961

William F. Buckley, Jr., *Up from Liberalism*, McDowell, Obolensky, New York, 1959

Edmund Cahn, *The Predicament of Democratic Man*, The Macmillan Company, New York, 1961

Norman Thomas, *A Socialist's Faith*, W. R. Norton and Company, Inc., New York, 1951

James D. Atkinson, *The Edge of War*, Henry Regnery Company, Chicago

Clausewitz, Karl von, *On War*

INDEX

191

ABOUT THE AUTHOR

SENATOR BARRY M. GOLDWATER, born on January 1, 1909, in Phoenix, Arizona, distinguished himself in the Air Force (he is now a brigadier general) and in his family's department store in Phoenix (he is now Chairman of the Board) before going into politics and getting himself elected to the United States Senate in 1953. Since 1953 he has become the acknowledged leader of the conservative wing of the Republican Party and is considered today to be one of the two or three outstanding candidates for the Republican nomination for the Presidency in 1964.

In what spare time he can find, Senator Goldwater is a flier, an amateur photographer of considerable skill, a writer, and an ardent family man (two girls and two boys). His earlier book, *The Conscience of a Conservative,* published in 1960, sold over a million copies in all editions.